Wonders of
WILDLIFE

Walt Disney Studios

Wonders of
WILDLIFE

Introduction
to
Animals

Grolier Enterprises Corp.

Cover: Male king penguin caring for egg.
Facing title page: Saw-whet owl.
Right: Sandhill crane.
Contents Page: Cecropia moth laying eggs.

Grolier Incorporated
PRESIDENT AND CHAIRMAN OF THE BOARD: Robert B. Clarke
VICE PRESIDENT, DIRECTOR OF MANUFACTURING: Dale E. Bowman
MANAGER, MAIL ORDER MANUFACTURING: David Bonjour
MANAGER, PRE-PRESS SERVICES: Tony Qureshi

Grolier Enterprises Corp.
PRESIDENT AND PUBLISHER: Robert W. Schramke
ASSOCIATE PUBLISHER: Henry J. Lefcort
EDITORIAL DIRECTOR: Ernest Kohlmetz
PUBLICATIONS COORDINATOR: Margaret Loos

Written by Jenny E. Tesar

Advisory Board

Dr. Richard G. Van Gelder, Curator, Department of Mammalogy, American Museum of Natural History

Dr. James W. Atz, Curator, Department of Ichthyology, American Museum of Natural History

Dr. Charles J. Cole, Curator, Department of Herpetology, American Museum of Natural History

Mr. Gary Hevel, Collections Manager, Department of Entomology, National Museum of Natural History, Smithsonian Institution

Dr. Duane Hope, Chairman, Department of Invertebrate Zoology, National Museum of Natural History, Smithsonian Institution

Dr. Noble S. Proctor, Assistant Professor of Biology, Southern Connecticut State College

Series Consultant: Jenny E. Tesar
Design: Kirchoff/Wohlberg, Inc.
Photo Research: Judith Greene

Walt Disney Productions
VICE PRESIDENT-PUBLISHING: Vincent Jefferds

ISBN 0-7172-8155-8
Library of Congress Catalog Number 79-67696

©1980 Walt Disney Productions

Printed in the United States of America

123453210

Contents

The World Of Animals

Zebras and wildebeests graze on the Serengeti Plain of Tanzania in East Africa. Moving among these large animals are cattle egrets. These birds watch for and then eat insects disturbed by the movements of the zebras and wildebeests. Although we cannot see them, other animals are also a part of this scene. Mice scurry through the grass. Ants carry bits of debris toward their nests. Perhaps a stalking lioness is hiding behind a screen of bushes, waiting for one of the zebras or wildebeests to stray away from its herd. Every one of these animals is different from every other animal. Yet they all have the same goal: survival.

One of the most wonderful and fascinating aspects of nature is the way that each animal is equipped to survive in its world. Each must obtain food and shelter and the other necessities of life. Each must be able to withstand attacks by its enemies. But what variety exists in the way that these needs are met! There are so many different types of food, homes, and weapons. There are different structures for moving from place to place, different colorations, different means of sensing changes in the environment. Some animals live on prairies while others live in treetops or buried in the ground. Some live in oceans or rivers while others make their homes in caves or on rocky Arctic islands.

Consider, too, the variety of behavior—how animals react to their mates, their offspring, other friendly animals or their enemies. Some animals live together in large groups while others live alone. Some animals remain in one place all year round while others migrate great distances every spring and fall.

Since prehistoric times, people have tried to understand the ways of animals. Many mysteries remain to be solved by the scientists of today and tomorrow. But many other secrets of the animal world have been uncovered. It is these facts, these wonders of wildlife, that amaze and fascinate us. This book deals in part with animals that we come into contact with in our daily lives and in part with exotic creatures that live in remote lands. As a whole, it creates a picture of the remarkable variety and adaptability of the animal world.

Wildebeests, zebras, and cattle egrets live in harmony on the Serengeti Plain of Tanzania in equatorial East Africa. Such natural scenes grow rarer as human civilization advances.

9

Each Animal is Unique

More than 1 million kinds of animals live on our planet. They come in every size, shape, and color. Some are so small that they can only be seen through a microscope. Others are bigger than a house. Each is unique—different in some way from every other kind of animal.

One feature that makes the blue whale unique is its size. It may be 100 feet long and weigh 150 tons. This is much larger than any dinosaur ever was or than any elephant ever is. In fact, it equals the combined weight of 2,000 average-sized men!

You might suppose that so large an animal would eat other large animals. But the blue whale feeds mostly on krill, tiny shrimplike animals that rarely are more than 3 inches long from the tip of their antennae to the end of their tails.

One of the cheetah's unique features is its speed. The cheetah can move faster than any other four-legged animal. As the cheetah rushes toward its prey, it may reach a speed of 70 miles per hour. The marlin is one of the fastest animals of the sea. This fish, sometimes called the "greyhound of the sea," can move through the water at speeds of more than 40 miles an hour. Among the fastest animals in the air is the peregrine falcon. This type of hawk preys mostly on smaller birds, capturing its victims while in flight. Peregrine falcons have been clocked at speeds

Speed is important to many animals. The **peregrine falcon** in the air, the **cheetah** on land, and the **marlin** in the sea all use their great speed in capturing prey.

The blue whale is so big that it is hard to imagine its size. One-fourth again as large as and five times heavier than the biggest dinosaur, brontosaurus, it dwarfs the elephant, the largest land-dwelling animal still in existence.

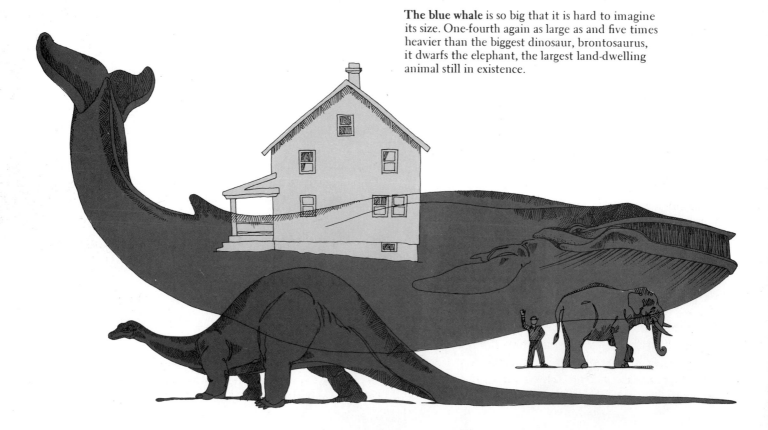

of more than 120 miles per hour when diving to capture prey.

The giraffe's height is one of the features that makes this animal unique. Some giraffes stand 17 feet tall. A third of this height is neck. The giraffe's neck contains only seven bones—the same seven bones that are found in the human neck, though the giraffe's neck bones are obviously much longer. The giraffe also has a big heart, which it needs for pumping blood up its long neck and into its head. It also has a special system for controlling blood pressure. When the giraffe bends down to drink at a water hole, the blood pressure decreases, so that blood does not rush into its head.

Blue whales, krill, cheetahs, marlins, peregrine falcons, giraffes. These are only half-a-dozen of the animals known to us. Add to these butterflies and starfish, earthworms and lobsters, snails and snakes, monkeys and magpies, and many, many others. In fact, the list gets longer every year. Scientists are continually discovering new and unique animals that they hadn't known existed before. For example, in 1977 scientists exploring in a deep-diving submarine discovered a giant worm living in cracks on the floor of the Pacific Ocean. It is found 8,000 feet below the water's surface—an environment that is always dark. This worm has no eyes, mouth, or digestive system. On its head is a feathery plume, which apparently is used to absorb food substances from the water. With the discovery of this strange worm, one more type of animal was added to the million-plus list of animals known to live on this planet.

A giant worm, never seen before, was recovered from the floor of the Pacific Ocean in 1977. The worm, which is 8.5 feet long and lives in a 1-inch diameter tube, is pink with a brilliant red tip.

Understanding Animals

People have always watched animals and tried to understand their behavior. Prehistoric hunters watched how animals ran, flew, and swam in order to find the easiest way to catch them. African hunters learned, for example, that hippos try to escape by running into water and that birds fly toward the light. They learned which animals would fight if trapped and how they fought. They learned when birds nested and where, so that they could gather eggs for food. They learned at what time of year fish swam upstream to lay eggs, so they could catch the fish when they were the most accessible.

Over the centuries people learned a great deal about animal behavior. Much of this has been put to practical use. For example, American Indians along the Pacific Northwest coast discovered that certain clams burrow deep into the muddy sand exposed during low tide to avoid being dried out by the air and sun. The clams are called gweducs (goo-ee-duks), which comes from an Indian word meaning "to dig deep." A gweduc has a long tube that reaches to the surface of the mud. Through this tube the gweduc gets rid of water from which it has taken out oxygen and food. It also uses the tube to take in a fresh supply of water. When the tube becomes exposed at low tide or when anything touches it, the gweduc quickly withdraws it into the mud.

People have learned how to gather the large, tasty gweducs while the mud flats are still covered with water. They watch for the little fountain that spouts forth from the tube as the clam expels water. Then the people quickly dig into the mud. Although the tube disappears at the first touch of the shovel against the mud, if the people have a good eye and dig deeply enough—perhaps 2 or 3 feet—they will find this giant clam.

Prehistoric people eventually learned how to tame, or domesticate, certain animals—cattle, pigs, horses, goats, and sheep. Some of these animals were raised as sources of food and clothing. Others were work animals that pulled or carried heavy loads and did other chores. Understanding the behavior of domesticated animals became as important as understanding the behavior of wild animals. For example, understanding the eating habits of horses is of practical value to people who raise horses. Horses eat all day long, but eat only a little food at a time. If a horse eats a lot of food all at once or eats too quickly, its small stomach becomes enlarged and the horse gets a painful stomach ache. The horse's in-

This curious cat risks double trouble—from the chair's rocker and from the electrical wire.

Gweducs are the largest clams in North America. One of these giant clams may weigh 16 pounds.

digestion becomes even worse if it drinks water after eating. People who raise horses make certain that their horses get only limited amounts of water and that they get this water before rather than after their meals.

Besides domesticated animals that help to make our lives easier, people also have pets that give them pleasure. If you want to have a healthy, happy pet, you must understand the behavior of that type of animal. "Curiosity killed the cat" is an old saying with much truth in it. Cats will investigate everything, including such dangerous objects as sewing baskets, electrical cords, and the insides of washing machines and clothes dryers. A smart cat owner makes certain that the home is a safe place for a curious cat.

People must also understand the behavior of animals that may be harmful to them. From household pests such as cockroaches and silverfish to carriers of disease such as malarial mosquitoes to venomous snakes and killer sharks—people must learn to control or to avoid animals that pose a direct threat to their comfort and well-being.

But what of the hundreds of thousands of animals that are neither sources of food, domesticated animals, pets, pests, nor direct threats to us? Why are we also interested in understanding their behavior? There are several reasons. For one, by better understanding the animal world, of which we too are members, we better understand ourselves. We obtain a clearer picture of where we fit into the whole scheme of life on this planet. We also gain a clearer appreciation of the extraordinary miracles of nature that are constantly occurring. Finally, we are building up a storehouse of knowledge that someday may help us in improving our own lives and the world around us.

Sometimes animal behavior is easily observed by people, but its meaning is not immediately understood by them. For example, black-headed gulls nest in dense colonies in which the birds are so close together that they can almost touch one another. Why do the gulls nest in this way?

The nests of black-headed gulls are frequently attacked by herring gulls, which eat the eggs. If herring gulls approach the colony, all the black-headed gulls fly up and defend their nests. The greater the number of black-headed gulls, the less chance the herring gulls have of grabbing some of the eggs. Such mutual protection can be very valuable. Birds that nest on the outer edges of the colony may lose three times as many eggs to the attackers as the birds that nest in the crowded center.

Herring gulls are found in great numbers along the Atlantic coasts of both North America and Europe and along the Mediterranean coasts.

A black-headed gull sits on three eggs at a time. These are spotted or blotched—a pattern of brown and olive-gray that blends in with the nest and ground, making the eggs difficult to spot by the herring gulls. But when the first chick hatches, the white inside of its broken shell reflects the sunlight. Seeing this, the herring gulls know that there may be unhatched eggs nearby. Herring gulls also catch and eat chicks. The black-headed gull fools the herring gull by removing the shells from the nest shortly after the chicks are hatched. By pushing the broken shells away, the mother improves the chances that her eggs or chicks will avoid becoming another animal's dinner.

The black-headed gull, one of the smaller types of seagulls, is the most common gull in Europe.

Just as an animal's behavior must be understood to be appreciated, so must the animal's structure and physical capabilities. Every animal is well equipped for the life it leads. For example, the trunk of an elephant may seem like an odd structure, but it is at least as useful to the elephant as your arms and hands are to you. As much as six feet or more in length and containing thousands of muscles, the elephant's trunk is sensitive and flexible. The elephant uses its trunk to strip leaves from a plant, to pick up food from the ground, and to carry food to its mouth. By curling its trunk around an object, the elephant can pick up very heavy objects, including logs that weigh several hundred pounds.

The elephant's trunk is formed from its nose and upper lip. At the tip of the trunk are the nostrils. The elephant has a very sharp sense of smell, which tells it that an enemy or some tasty food is nearby. Also at the far end of the African elephant's trunk are two fingerlike projections. One is located on top of the trunk above the nostrils, the other is on the underside. These act like sensitive fingers and are capable of picking up an object as small as a peanut.

Elephants enjoy taking baths—either wet baths in muddy water or dry baths in dust or sand. They suck up the water or dust in their trunks, then blow it over their bodies. The elephant drinks water in a similar manner. It dips the tip of its trunk into a river or lake and sucks up several gallons of water. It then squirts the water into its mouth. An elephant may drink as much as 40 gallons of water a day.

The elephant's trunk also can be used as a weapon of defense or as a fly swatter. It can be used to examine an unfamiliar object or to push a reluctant young elephant up a hill. It truly is a marvelous structure.

Elephants take frequent water and dust baths to protect and cool their thick but sensitive skins and flush bothersome insects from the skin folds.

The elephant's trunk should be approached with caution. Angry or startled elephants have used their trunks to seize and injure people.

An elephant uses its trunk to pull the leaves from a tree and stuff them into its mouth. It will sometimes strip a whole tree.

The very different structure of the stonefish also is fascinating. This small fish, which lives in coral reefs in the Indian and Pacific oceans, gets its name from the fact that it blends in with surrounding rocks and can lie very still for long periods of time. But even more interesting is the fact that it is the most venomous fish known. On its upper surface are spines that connect to venom glands. One milligram of the stonefish's venom can kill 100 mice. (A postage stamp weighs 65 milligrams.) A single stonefish ten inches long could produce enough venom to kill more than 30,000 mice. However, the stonefish almost never uses its spines and venom to capture food. So why does it have such a deadly system? The most obvious reason is defense. But no one has tested stonefish venom against other fish. That's the unknown. In the world of animals, however, scientists believe that everything is done and everything exists for a reason. By discovering these reasons, we better understand the world of animals.

The stonefish blends into its surroundings. It can remain very still for long periods of time.

Animals Live Everywhere

High on a mountain in western Canada, a swarm of springtails forms a golden carpet on the snow. Deep in the Pacific, in a world where sunlight never reaches, fish with built-in lights hunt for food. In the Arizona desert, a rattlesnake slithers beneath a rock ledge to escape the noonday sun. In a city gutter, rainwater carries tiny one-celled animals toward the sewer. In a Brazilian rain forest, a group of monkeys settle down to feed on ripe figs.

Everywhere on this planet there are animals: on land, in the air, in fresh water and salt water, in caves and treetops, even inside other animals. The place where an animal lives is called its habitat. Each kind of animal has a particular habitat to which it is best adapted.

Your home may be an example of a habitat. It is only part of your habitat. But it may be the entire habitat of a cat, dog, parakeet, or other indoor pet. Most people are willing to share their homes with such animals. We are not so willing to share our homes with other animals that find houses and apartments ideal habitats—pests such as ants, cockroaches, house mice, silverfish, and termites.

A tidal pool is an example of a very different habitat. Sea anemones (uh-NEM-o-neez), flower-shaped relatives of coral, fill the cracks. Small fish swim around, avoiding the tentacles of the sea anemones. Starfish move slowly over the rocks. Crabs scurry about. Barnacles, clinging to the rocks, open and close their shells. Each of these animals is built so it can survive in the tidal pool. It behaves in such a way that it can meet all its needs in this habitat. Place it in another habitat and it would soon die.

The number of animals that live in any single habitat can be enormous. For example, some 200 acres of sagebrush country in the western United States may contain several thousand rodents, a few dozen rabbits, plus some badgers, pronghorn antelopes, and bats. Add to this list insects, birds, and other animals that live in the area and you can see that even land as barren as sagebrush country supports a great deal of life.

Generally, in any habitat there are greater numbers of smaller kinds of animals than there are larger animals. The soil of an acre of forest land may be home for 700 million tiny mites. In contrast, a single bear may range through a forest covering dozens of acres.

Some kinds of animals are found over a wide

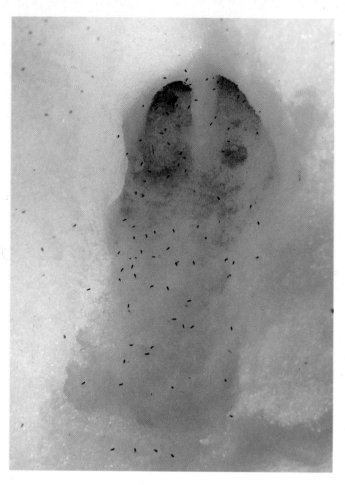

A swarm of springtails (snow fleas) gather in a track left by a passing deer.

area of the world. Other animals are found in only limited areas. Many animals that live in the ocean are found the world over. Killer whales, pilot whales, and blue whales live in all the seas of the world—or did, until people's overhunting greatly decreased their numbers. Certain tiny animals also live in all the oceans of the world. These microscopic animals form part of the plankton, the floating mass of animal and plant life on which all the animals of the ocean depend for food, either directly or indirectly.

On land, animals that live in temperate climates, such as that in most of the United States, tend to be widespread. For example, deer mice are found throughout North America, in almost every kind of habitat. Some live in woods, others live in fields, still others live in barns or under houses. The snowshoe rabbit also is found in many areas, living in Colorado mountain forests and near the Rhode Island seashore, in Alaskan meadows and West Virginian marshes.

Starfish and sea anemones live in this tidal pool on the coast of the state of Washington.

Cave-dwelling bats live in similar habitats as far apart as Bali in Indonesia and Kentucky.

But other animals have very limited habitats. The pothole mosquito lives only in potholes—small temporary pools in rock depressions—in the desert of the American southwest. For months at a time, the depression is a dry, sandy pit. But after a rainstorm fills it with water, it comes to life: fairy shrimp, tadpole shrimp, clam shrimp, certain aquatic beetles, and pothole mosquitoes suddenly appear. Where do they come from?

During the dry period, they survived as eggs lying in the sand. When water fills the potholes, the eggs hatch. The young mosquitoes develop quickly. Less than six days after birth, they are adults. The females fly off in search of males with which to mate and, after that, a warm-blooded animal to bite. The blood the female takes from the victim will provide food for the eggs she lays at the edge of the already drying pothole—eggs that will hatch after the next rainstorm.

Where similar habitats exist in different parts of the world, they tend to be home to similar kinds of animals. The rocks of tidal pools all around North America are home for periwinkles, small animals with spiral shells. The periwinkles that live along the Atlantic coast, the Gulf of Mexico, and the Pacific coast are all built very much alike and feed on the same kinds of plants. Similarly, the ocean bottom off the northeastern coast is home for the lobster; off the Gulf coast is found the stone crab; off the Pacific, the king crab. All three are large shellfish that feed on dead animal matter.

18

A forest fire in Glacier National Park, Montana,
left many animals dead or destroyed their homes.

These dinosaur tracks in southern Africa were
made some 150 million years ago. They are
preserved in stone.

Habitats may change. A forest may burn down. A meadow may be flooded. A family may put an ant-killing powder in the kitchen closets. When this happens, the animals that live in the habitat must react. Sometimes the animals can adjust to the changes or move elsewhere. Sometimes they cannot. If they cannot, they die. If all the animals of any single type die, then that animal will never again be seen on earth. It has become extinct.

The history of our planet is filled with stories of animals that could not adjust to changes in their habitats. Some, such as the elephant bird and the northern sea cow, became extinct rather recently. Others, such as the dinosaurs, died out millions of years ago. We know of them only by the remains or traces they left behind.

What is an Animal?

No one would mistake a cottonmouth for anything other than a snake. Like all snakes it has a long, narrow, limbless body. Nor would anyone have trouble recognizing the cottonmouth as an animal. Most people would point to its head with two eyes, its ability to move, and its capture of other animals for food as proof of its membership in the animal world.

In contrast, no one would say that cotton is an animal. One look at it says it is a plant. It has green leaves, branches, roots, and, before the cotton bolls form, delicate creamy-white flowers.

What about sea cucumbers and sea fans? They don't have heads with two eyes. Nor do they have green leaves. Are they animals or plants? And what about sponges, corals, and comb jellies?

A cottonmouth snake could never be confused with a cotton plant even though the snake's open mouth is as round and white as a puff of cotton.

Before discussing the differences between animals and plants, let's consider an even more basic question: what is life? Over the centuries, many people have tried to answer this question. However, no simple answer has yet been found. It may be that such an answer does not exist.

What can be done, however, is to describe some of the basic features of living things—features that set them apart from non-living objects. Five major features are: the ability to turn food into energy (metabolism), a definite size and shape (structure), the ability to respond to changes (sensitivity), a definite life cycle, and the ability to reproduce.

Without the ability to turn food into energy, no animal or plant could survive. It could not move, grow, repair itself, reproduce, or carry on any other activity.

Every living thing has a definite size range and, usually, a more or less fixed shape. An elephant, a cottonmouth, and a cotton plant are easily recognized because of their distinctive shapes. In contrast, the shape of nonliving objects such as soil, sand, and water can be changed without changing the objects themselves.

Every living thing responds to changes in its environment. This feature is called sensitivity. The changes—in light, sound, moisture, heat, and so on—are called stimuli (singular: stimulus). An animal or plant may respond by changing. Or it may respond by moving toward or away from the stimulus. For example, you may respond to loud noises by getting a headache or an earache. Or you may respond by moving away from the noise. If the noises are pleasant ones, you may respond by smiling or clapping your hands.

Every living thing has a definite life cycle. It is born, it grows, it matures, it ages, it dies. It does not live forever but has a definite life span. How long it lives depends on the type of plant or animal it is. Certain microscopic plants and animals live for no more than a few hours. Some insects live for only a few weeks. Some plants, called annuals, live for only one season. At the other end of the scale are such long-living trees as the giant sequoia, which may live for as long as 2,500 years. Very few animals live as long as 100 years.

Living things are able to produce more living things of the same kind. This is called reproduction. When a cottonmouth reproduces, baby cottonmouths are created. If the cottonmouth does not reproduce, its characteristics aren't passed on to a new generation. If all the cottonmouths do not reproduce, or if their rate of reproduction is less than the rate at which older cottonmouths die, the animals will become extinct—there will no longer be cottonmouths on earth.

Although plants and animals share these five basic features—metabolism, structure, sensitivity, life cycle, and reproduction—there are differences between plants and animals that separate them into the plant world and the animal world.

To begin with, most plants can make their own food through the process called photosynthesis (fo-tow-SIN-tha-sis). These plants contain the green pigment chlorophyll (KLOR-a-fil) in their cells that is used in making food. Animal cells do not contain chlorophyll, so animals cannot make their own food. Animals must obtain their food by eating plants and/or other animals. The cottonmouth, for example, catches and eats fish, frogs, and other small animals.

The cell is the basic unit of all plants and animals. One of the main differences between plants and animals is in the structure of the cell. Plant cells are surrounded by a wall made of material called cellulose. Animal cells are not surrounded by a cell wall, but a delicate cell membrane.

The giant tortoise, which is the largest of all tortoises, is one of only a few animals that may live for more than 100 years.

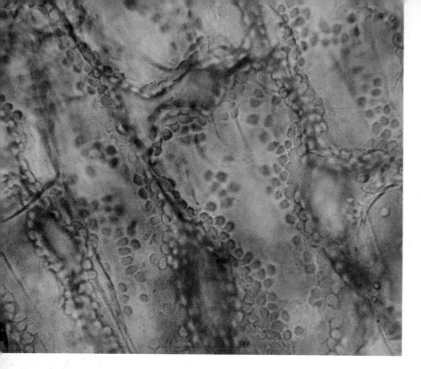

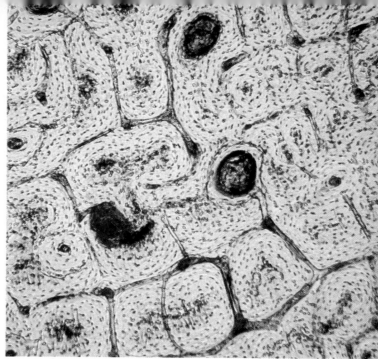

Plant cells, such as these tulip cells, usually contain their chlorophyll in round bodies called chloroplasts. Notice the thick cellulose walls.

Animal cells, such as these mammalian bone cells, do not have thick cellulose walls like most plant cells. But notice the dark nuclei.

An animal has a much more definite size and shape than does a plant. A cottonmouth always has one head, two eyes, a length not exceeding 6½ feet, and so on. But a cotton plant may be 3 feet or 8 feet high. It may have 100 leaves or 300 leaves, 5 flowers or 40 flowers—or any number in between.

In general, animals react more quickly to stimuli than plants do. If a bright light is shone toward a cottonmouth, the snake will immediately turn away or decrease the size of the pupils of its eyes. A cotton plant also will turn toward or away from the light, but it will take a day or more to do so. One plant that does react quickly is the Venus flytrap. If an insect lands on one of its leaves, the plant reacts by folding the two halves of the leaf together. This takes less than a second.

One final distinction between plants and animals concerns movement. Animals have the ability to move from one place to another, at least during some part of their lives. Most plants do not have this ability. A cottonmouth can swim quickly through the lake in which it lives. A cotton plant remains forever where its seed was sown.

All living things can be classified as either plants or animals. Usually it is easy to tell the difference between a plant and an animal. But when it is not so easy, scientists must look closely at the five basic features of living things and at the differences in these features as they occur in the plant world and the animal world.

A Venus flytrap takes less than a second to trap an insect but up to 10 days to digest it. In its short life it may eat only three or four victims.

22

What's in a Name?

"I saw a cougar last week," said Joe. "That sure is a big cat!"

"We've got mountain lions where we live," said Anna. "They're the biggest cats in North America."

"No they aren't," replied Carol. "Pumas are the biggest cats on the continent."

If these three people are lucky, a fourth person in the group will tell them that they are all talking about the same animal.

It is only natural for people to give names to animals they observe. But problems arise when different people give different names to the same animals. So scientists who study animals have worked out a system of grouping and naming animals based on their structures. No two animals that are different in structure share the same full scientific names.

The scientific names for animals are based on Greek and Latin, two languages that once were used by scientists in many countries. The scientific name for any animal has two basic parts—its genus name, which is the general category to which the animal belongs, and its species name, a more specific category to which the animal belongs. (Remember: *gen*us, general; *speci*es, specific.) For example, both the mountain lion and the house cat are members of the genus *Felis*. But a mountain lion's complete name is *Felis concolor*. A house cat is *Felis domestica*. An ordinary pet dog is *Canis familiaris*, a coyote is *Canis latrans*, a wolf is *Canis lupus*. They all belong to the genus *Canis*, but each is a different species.

Scientific names are usually chosen for much the same reasons as are common names. Anteaters are so-called because they eat ants. Scientists have given them the genus name *Myrmecophaga*, which comes from the Greek words meaning "ant eater."

The species part of the name usually describes some feature of the animal. For example, the slow-worm, a lizard with a tail that is fragile (easily breaks off) is called *Anguis fragilis*. A weasel that lives in Patagonia (southern Argentina) is called *Lyncodon patagonicus*. Locusts that migrate are called *Locusta migratoria*. And the starling, one of the commonest of birds, is called *Sturnus vulgaris* (*vulgar* is a Latin word that means "common").

Most of the time in this book, and in all the books in this series, the common name of animals will be used. But some animals are so seldom noticed by people that they do not have common names! Other times, the scientific name must be given because more than one animal shares the common name.

Cougar, mountain lion, puma, catamount . . . are different names for the same cat, *Felis concolor*.

The Major Groups of Animals

All pet cats—be they Domestic Shorthairs, Persians, Siamese—share the scientific name *Felis domestica*. Domestic Shorthair, Persian, Siamese are all breeds, a smaller, more particular category of pet cats. All *Felis domestica*, together with all other cats, belong to the family Felidae. A family is a broader category than a genus. Other families include the bear family (Ursidae) and the dog family (Canidae). All three of these families belong to a broader category, the order Carnivora. All carnivores are meat-eaters belonging to the still broader category, the class Mammalia. Finally, all mammals belong to the phylum (plural: phyla) Chordata, which includes all animals with backbones.

The chart on the next two pages lists the ten major phyla of the animal world. It begins with the simplest animals and ends with the most complex. The chart explains what the name of each phylum means, lists major features of each phylum, and gives examples of animals in each phylum.

The Major Groups of Animals

Phylum	Major Features
Protozoa (pro-toe-ZOE-a) "First animals"	One-celled mostly microscopic animals. Found on land and in fresh and marine waters.
Porifera (poe-RIF-er-a) "Pore-bearing animals"	The simplest of the many-celled animals. Many pores in the body wall of the saclike body connect the central cavity to the outside. Found in fresh and marine waters.
Coelenterata (si-len-te-RAY-ta) "Animals with hollow intestines"	The simplest animals with cells organized into tissues. They have tentacles and stinging cells. Many live in colonies. Found in fresh and marine waters.
Platyhelminthes (plat-ee-hel-MIN-theez) "Flat worms"	Soft, flat, unsegmented worms. Some live in fresh water. Most live in other animals.
Aschelminthes (ask-hel-MIN-theez) "Sac worms"	Small worms with round, often elongated bodies. Found on land and in fresh and marine waters.
Annelida (a-NEL-i-da) "Ringed animals"	Slender, segmented worms. Many species have paired appendages on most of the segments. Found on land and in fresh and marine waters.
Echinodermata (eh-kee-no-DUR-ma-ta) "Spiny-skinned animals"	Body usually has five arms. Tube feet are used for movement. A skeleton of hard plates is embedded in the skin and may bear spines. Found in marine waters.
Mollusca (ma-LUS-ka) "Soft-bodied animals"	Soft-bodied animals, usually covered by a shell. The entire body is enclosed in a tissue called the mantel. They have a footlike appendage, which takes different forms. Most are marine but some live on land or in fresh water.
Arthropoda (ar-THROP-a-da) "Joint-footed animals"	The body is divided into segments. Appendages are jointed. Body and appendages are usually covered by a hard outer skeleton, which sheds as the animal grows. Found on land, in the air, and in fresh and marine waters.
Chordata (core-DAY-ta) "Animals with notochord"	The most highly developed animals. They have a flexible rodlike structure, the notochord, which in some members (the vertebrates) is replaced by a more complex backbone. Vertebrates have an internal skeleton and a well-developed brain. Most chordates have 2 pairs of jointed limbs — either fins or legs. Found on land, in the air, and in fresh and marine waters.

Examples	
Amoeba, euglena, paramecium, volvox	
Sponges	
Hydra, jellyfish, Portuguese man-of-war, coral, sea anemone	
Planaria, fluke, tapeworm	
Rotifer, roundworm, hookworm, vinegar eel	
Sandworm, earthworm, leech	
Starfish, sea urchin, sand dollar, sea cucumber	
Oyster, clam, scallop, snail, slug, squid, octopus, nautilus	
Crustaceans (crab, lobster, barnacle), spider, scorpion, centipede, millipede, insects	
Fish, amphibians, reptiles, birds, mammals	

25

What Animals Eat

During the night a spider built a large but delicate-looking web between two branches of a bush bordering a suburban lawn. Now, as the dew that collected on the web evaporates, the spider waits. It lies quietly in the center of the web. And waits.

In midmorning a grasshopper, its belly half filled with grass, lands in the spider web. The sticky web holds the grasshopper. As it tries to free itself, its legs become tangled in the threads of the web.

The spider, which began moving toward the grasshopper as soon as it touched the web, is now upon its victim. It bites the grasshopper, injecting venom into the insect's body. Next, the spider enmeshes the grasshopper in silk threads. Soon the grasshopper is dead. The spider begins to eat its meal.

But the spider barely begins to eat when a bluebird swoops down and catches the spider. This same bluebird has already caught a grasshopper and eaten some berries.

If it is unlucky, the bluebird will become a meal for the neighborhood cat. If it is lucky, it will die of old age. Its decaying body, lying at the base of a tree, will then be eaten by carrion beetles and other insects.

All animals must eat to live. What an animal eats depends on what kind of animal it is. The spider doesn't eat grass—and the grasshopper doesn't eat spiders. The bluebird eats many types of foods, none of which are eaten by a carrion beetle.

A spider builds a web. The web may entangle a **grasshopper**. But before the spider can enjoy its meal, both spider and grasshopper may be eaten by a hungry **bluebird**.

The Kaibab Plateau, near the Grand Canyon in northern Arizona, had a delicate balance of animals and plants. When the deer became too numerous for the food supply, many of them starved.

Some animals, such as most grasshoppers, eat only plant matter. There are microscopic plant-eaters and plant-eaters that weigh a ton or more. Land snails, potato beetles, and elephants are examples of plant-eaters. The scientific name for plant-eaters is herbivores (which means "grass-eaters").

Animals, such as the spider, that eat other animals are called predators. Jellyfish, bald eagles, and killer whales are all examples of predators. Predators play a very important role in the world. They keep down the number of plant-eaters. Without predators, plant-eaters would so increase in numbers that they would eat all the plant life. With all the plant life gone, there would be no more food for the plant-eaters. They would all die. In the long run, the earth would cease to contain anything that lived.

People learned this truth in harsh ways. One famous lesson took place in Arizona early in this century. There, on the Kaibab Plateau, lived many types of green plants. Deer fed on the plants. Wolves, mountain lions, and coyotes fed on the deer.

About 4,000 deer lived on the Kaibab Plateau. For centuries the number of deer had remained about the same. Although some of the deer fell victim to predators, new deer were born. But people did not like the idea of deer being killed by predators. In 1906, when the Kaibab Plateau was made a national game reserve, the government started a campaign to kill the predators. Money was offered to anyone who killed a wolf, coyote, or mountain lion. In the next two decades, thousands of predators were trapped or shot. As the number of predators decreased, the number of deer increased. By 1924 there were 100,000 deer on the Kaibab Plateau. The plateau did not have enough plant life to support such a large deer population. The deer began to starve. Their slow death by starvation must surely have been much more painful than the quick death inflicted by a predator.

Shocked by conditions, the government again intervened. Hunting permits were issued, allowing license holders to kill deer. Over a 5-year period hunters killed about 5,000 deer—a small number in comparison with the 96,000 that died of starvation in just two years. Today, the Kaibab Plateau has regained its beauty. And, in that part which is a National Forest, neither deer nor their predators may be disturbed by people.

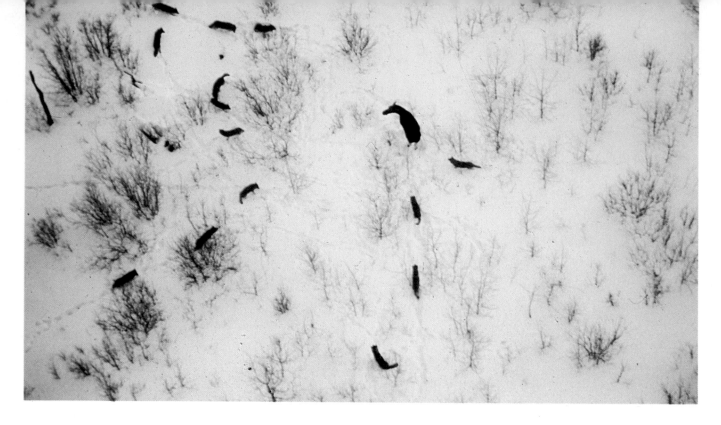

A lone **moose** is surrounded by wolves. The wolves work together to block any escape route. If the moose is killed, the wolves will probably fight over the meat.

Being a predator is hard work. Most attempts by a predator to catch and kill prey fail. One scientist, L. David Mech, studied a pack of wolves that lived on Isle Royale, an island in Lake Superior. He watched them hunt moose a total of 131 times. On 54 of these times the wolves didn't even get close to the moose. On the remaining 77 times the wolves were able to attack the moose. But in these 77 attacks only 6 moose were killed. And in these 6 cases, the moose caught by the wolves was either very young, very old, sick, or injured. The strongest, healthiest, most alert moose held their own against the wolves.

Some animals eat both plants and animals. They are called omnivores ("all eaters"). The bluebird is an omnivore. So are raccoons, foxes, and skunks. The brown rat is perhaps the most omnivorous of all animals. It eats lizards, birds, insects, spiders, fruits, vegetables, seeds, garbage, and even other brown rats.

The ability to eat many types of food is a great advantage. If one food is scarce, the animal can eat something else. And the animal can eat foods that only are available at certain times of the year. For example, the grizzly bear of Alaska eats mostly roots in spring. In early summer it eats horsetails and reed grass. In late summer it feeds on berries and perhaps on salmon that have swum upriver to lay their eggs. In all seasons the grizzly bear chases and catches ground squirrels.

Some animals eat plants during one stage of their lives and other animals during another stage. Immature blister beetles eat other insects; adult blister beetles feed on plants. Bullfrog tadpoles eat microscopic plants and bacteria. Adult bullfrogs eat insects, small fish, snakes, mice, birds, and so on—in other words, almost any animal they can catch. The caterpillar of the promethea moth eats the leaves of cherry, maple, and other trees and bushes. The adult moth, like many other adult moths, does not eat at all!

Animals such as the carrion beetle are called scavengers. They feed on the meat of dead animals, either those that died natural deaths or that were killed by predators. The coyote is both a predator and a scavenger. It may chase and kill an animal itself. Or it may eat the remains of another predator's dinner.

Some scientists believe that the earliest people were scavengers. According to this theory, our prehistoric ancestors ate the leftovers of animals killed but only partially eaten by predators such as the saber-toothed tiger. Gradually, however, people invented ways to catch and kill their own meat.

Today people are the major predators on earth. We kill animals not only for food but also for clothing, medicine, and other useful materials. And, sometimes we kill animals just for sport—behavior rarely found among other predators of the animal world.

Adaptations for Survival

In order to survive, an animal must adapt to its environment, the world in which it lives. To adapt is to adjust successfully to one's environment.

There are three basic types of adaptations: structural, functional, and behavioral. Structural adaptations are based on how an animal is built. Functional adaptations are based on the ways in which an animal's internal systems (lungs, heart, kidneys, and so on) operate. Behavioral adaptations are based on all the things an animal does. Of course, all three types of adaptations interact within an animal.

For example, in order to grow, a termite must shed its skin. This is a structural adaptation. A termite cannot digest the wood it eats. It depends on fungi, protozoans, and bacteria living in its digestive tract to digest the food. This is a functional adaptation. When a termite sheds its skin, it also loses the part of its digestive system that contains the organisms needed to digest wood. To get them back, the termite eats the skin it just shed. This is a behavioral adaptation.

The interaction of the three types of adaptations also is evident in the northern pipefish. This fish is well named. It is long and skinny like a pipe. At the end of its tubelike snout is a small, toothless mouth.

The pipefish, which is about 8 inches long, lies in shallow water along the eastern coast of North America. It spends its life among seaweed and grasses that grow attached to the bottom. Sometimes it adopts a more-or-less vertical position, with its nose near the bottom. Its upright tail moves slowly with the water's currents. When living among red algae, it has a reddish color. When living among green algae, it has a greenish color.

These two adaptations to its world help protect the pipefish from its enemies. The first—appearing like a long blade of seaweed—is an example of mimicry. The second—adopting the color of its environment—is an example of camouflage.

To gather food, the pipefish has other adaptations. Its two eyes work independently of one another. Thus the fish can look two ways at once. (This helps the fish notice enemies, too.) The small, narrow mouth and snout are misleading. Both can be stretched, allowing the pipefish to swallow large prey.

To protect their eggs, pipefish have the same adaptations as their better-known relative, the sea horse. The male has a pouch on his belly. The female places her eggs in this pouch. After the young fish

The flamingo's beautiful long, arched neck; long, slender legs; and curving beak are all structural adaptations that help it to survive in its environment.

29

hatch, the male carries them until they are old enough to go off on their own. This ensures that not as many of the eggs and young will be eaten by predators as among species that do not exercise parental care.

Other adaptations enable the pipefish to swim in either a vertical (up and down) or a horizontal (back and forth) position. The fin on its back (dorsal fin) helps it maintain a vertical position. The tail is used to swim horizontally. The first is useful when the pipefish wants to stay more or less where it is. The second, or horizontal, motion is used when the pipefish wants to move quickly from one place to another.

Every animal has many adaptations that enable it to live efficiently in its environment. These same adaptations make it difficult if not impossible for the animal to live elsewhere. A pipefish's adaptations allow it to live successfully in its salty, plant-filled world. But it wouldn't survive in an environment without seaweeds and grasses to hide among. A polar

The pipefish is so structured that it can remain vertical—rightside up or upside down.

bear would not survive in the Arizona desert. And a rattlesnake would not survive the icy winters of the Canadian Arctic.

Different animals may have different adaptations for doing the same thing. A woolly monkey may use its tail to hold onto a tree branch. A robin uses its feet. To climb a tree a rat snake depends on overlapping plates, or scutes, on its belly. The mudskipper, a small fish of Southeast Asia, uses its fins to crawl over mudflats and to haul itself up tree trunks in search of food. A woodpecker uses its feet—with an assist from its tail.

To catch food, a bat depends on its echolocation system. A rattlesnake depends on its ability to detect heat. A lion depends on surprise.

The following three sections look more closely at some of the structural, functional, and behavioral adaptations found in the animal world.

Structural Adaptations

A horse gallops across the plains. A gecko scampers up a wall. A river otter swims underwater. A gibbon swings from tree to tree. A pocket gopher burrows into the ground. A grouse walks over snow.

All these animals are moving from one place to another. All are using their limbs. But how differently these limbs are built!

The horse, for all practical purposes, has only one toe on each foot. This toe is enclosed in a hard hoof. The hooves are designed to move over hard, flat surfaces. The gecko has many tiny suction disks on the botton of each toe. These enable the lizard to cling to almost any surface, no matter how steep or smooth. The hind feet of the river otter are large and webbed. The feet spread wide as the otter swims and propel the otter much like oars propel a rowboat. The gibbon uses its front limbs to move rapidly through the trees. It hooks the fingers of each front limb over a branch. The pocket gopher has sturdy feet and toes with long claws that can quickly move aside dirt. The grouse has a row of teethlike projections on each of its toes. These keep the bird from sinking into the snow.

Just as there are many different kinds of limbs among members of the animal world, there are many different kinds of eyes, mouths, skeletons, and so on. These are all structural adaptations.

The different types of limbs just described are adaptations for different lifestyles. So are the different types of mouth parts found among animals. Even among the mammals there is great diversity.

The canine teeth of a cat are much larger than the cat's other teeth. They form sharp fangs, which are used to stab and hold the prey. Four teeth at the back of the mouth—two on the upper jaw and two on the lower—have sharp bladelike edges. These are used to cut the meat.

The upper canines of a European wild boar have developed into long tusks that are used in fighting.

The anteater has no teeth. It picks up ants with its long sticky tongue and swallows them whole.

Many whales, such as the blue and Greenland whales, don't have teeth either. Instead, they have long, thin plates of a horny material set close together all around the upper jaw. This is baleen, or whalebone. In the Greenland whale, the baleen may weigh from 1,000 to 3,000 pounds. In feeding, the whale opens its mouth, takes in a huge gulp of water carrying krill, then closes its mouth. It forces the water out between the baleen plates. The frayed inner edges of the plates strain out the krill, which are then swallowed.

Animals that are very similar may be adapted to very different environments. For example, the Arctic fox, which lives near the North Pole, has tiny ears. The desert fox, which lives in the deserts of northern Africa, has huge ears. Why do these two foxes have very different ears?

Many blood vessels are located near the surface of an ear. Heat passes from the blood vessels through

A woodpecker, such as the West Indian red-bellied woodpecker shown here, has 12 especially strong tail feathers. The bird uses these to help support its body as it climbs trees.

The Arctic fox (below) changes to a white coat for the winter. The fennec fox (below right), a desert fox, remains white and sand-colored all year.

31

The **giant anteater** of tropical America eats ants, termites, and other insects. It can extend its sticky tongue 18 inches beyond its lips.

the skin to the outside. The larger the ears, the greater the animal's ability to lose heat. In the chilly Arctic, large ears would be a disadvantage. An Arctic animal needs to conserve as much body heat as it can. In a hot desert, the reverse is true. There, large ears are an advantage. They help an animal get rid of excess heat.

Another interesting structural difference is found among moles. The common American mole and the star-nosed mole both have thick bodies with a short neck and a long snout. Both have small,

The **star-nosed mole** thrives in swamplands. When it eats, it contracts the fingerlike appendages on its snout.

underdeveloped eyes. In both, the front feet are powerful spadelike structures adapted for digging. Both eat primarily earthworms and insects. Both live in eastern North America.

But when it comes to noses, the similarities end. The common mole has a pointed, rather ordinary-looking snout. The star-nosed mole's snout ends in a disk around which are 22 fleshy fingerlike appendages. As the star-nosed mole tunnels underground, the fingerlike appendages are in constant motion, helping the animal to feel its way.

Sometimes animals that are physically very different have adapted similarly to the same environment. Seals are mammals, yet their bodies are as streamlined as a fish's body. This enables them to move easily in their ocean environment. Bats also are mammals. But they have developed wings, enabling them to share the air with insects and birds.

Animals of the intertidal zone—the area at the edge of an ocean that is covered by water during high tide and exposed to the air during low tide—are adapted to the tides. Many have structures designed to resist the sudden rush of water at high tide. Mussels attach themselves to the rocks by means of small but strong threads. Oysters and barnacles cement themselves to firm surfaces. Other seashore animals are flattened to minimize friction between themselves and the breaking waves. Oysters are examples of this adaptation.

Functional Adaptations

A deep-sea diver must wear a diving suit through which he receives a constant supply of air. Without the oxygen in the air, he would quickly die.

As he dives deeper into the water, the pressure in his body increases. Because of the increased pressure, nitrogen from the air dissolves into the diver's blood and other body tissues.

When the diver is ready to return to the surface, he must come up slowly or in a special decompression chamber. Otherwise, the nitrogen that has dissolved in his body tissues will be released faster than his lungs can get rid of it. Bubbles of nitrogen will form in his blood. This can kill a diver. Or it can cause great pain—a condition known as the "bends."

Whales also dive deep into the ocean, often to even greater depths than those reached by people in diving suits. One sperm whale dove so deeply that it became entangled in an underwater telegraph cable off the Pacific Coast of South America. The cable was more than 3,700 feet below the surface.

Like people, sperm whales have lungs and they breathe in air. Yet they can stay under water for more

A whale must open its blowhole when it surfaces and close it when it submerges.

than an hour without refreshing their bodies' supply of oxygen. And when they return to the surface, they can do so quickly.

What functional adaptations allow whales to stay under the water at great depths for long periods of time and then return quickly to the surface?

The whale's supply of air is limited to what it has in its lungs at the time it dives. However, its lungs can take in a much greater proportion of fresh, oxygen-rich air than a person's lungs can. When you breathe in and out, only a small part of the stale, oxygen-poor air in your lungs is replaced. But whales breathe much more deeply, and so they take in much more oxygen.

Before diving, the whale breathes in and out several times. With each breathing in (inhalation), oxygen enters the lungs and passes into the blood. The breathing out (exhalation) is called "blowing," or "having the spoutings out." The blow, or spout, is a foam made up of water, oil, and air low in oxygen (oxygen-poor).

The muscles of a whale contain large quantities of myoglobin, a chemical that combines with oxygen. This enables a whale to store great amounts of oxygen in its body before it dives. The oxygen then is slowly released from the myoglobin while the whale is underwater.

After a final deep breath, the whale dives. Although its body is filled with oxygen, the only air and, therefore, the only nitrogen in the body is that in the lungs. This limited amount probably is not enough to cause bubbles to form in the whale's blood when it returns to the surface. The whale also has additional functional adaptations that help prevent the bends.

As the whale moves deep into the ocean, its lungs begin to collapse. This causes the lining of the lungs to thicken. As a result, the blood vessels in the lining of the lungs are further away from the air in the lungs and less likely to absorb nitrogen. The collapse of the lungs also forces air to pass from the lungs into the windpipe and passages leading to the blowhole. The lining of the passages does not contain many blood vessels. Thus little absorption of nitrogen can occur. Also, the passages connect with sacs filled with foam. The oil in the foam absorbs nitrogen, thereby storing it until the whale surfaces and blows.

One more functional adaptation should be mentioned. When the whale dives, the rate at which its heart beats (its pulse) drops. It beats only about half as fast as it does when the whale is on the surface. This means the blood moves more slowly through the body. Certain muscles also act to slow the movement of the blood. As a result, the tissues receive less oxygen. The only exception is the brain. It is kept well supplied with oxygen. If this weren't true, the whale would lose consciousness and die.

By the time the whale surfaces from a long dive, its body tissues are in great need of oxygen. The whale breathes in and out a number of times and soon replenishes its supply of oxygen.

The manner in which oxygen intake, nitrogen absorption, and heart beat are regulated by the whale are examples of functional adaptations. They are adjustments of basic life processes—in these examples, respiration and circulation of the blood.

The lungs of people and whales are very similar in structure. But as we have seen, these lungs function very differently. People and whales have similar hearts, but these hearts function very differently.

Another basic life process that animals must regulate is the amount of water in their bodies. People take in most of the water they need by drinking it. The kangaroo rat lives in deserts where there is often no free-standing water to drink. A person stranded in such a place would soon die of thirst. But the kangaroo rat gets all the water it needs from seeds and other plant matter that it eats. Like a person, its tissues produce wastes. These pass into the blood and to the kidneys, which remove the wastes from the body. Human kidneys need a lot of water to work properly. The kangaroo rat's kidneys need very little water to remove the wastes. A person's urine is largely water. A kangaroo rat's urine contains so little water that it turns into a solid minutes after it is eliminated.

Animals also must regulate their body temperature. Animals that are able to keep a constant body temperature are called warm-blooded. Only birds and mammals are warm-blooded. All other animals are called cold-blooded and are the temperature of their surroundings. Their body temperatures change when the outside temperature around them changes.

The bodies of people living in extremely cold climates have undergone certain functional changes that make the people better adapted to the harsh climate. The body tissues of people who live in the Arctic burn food faster than those of people who live in temperate climates, so they produce more heat. Also, Arctic people's hearts beat faster, sending more warm blood to the hands and feet.

Most living things try to avoid extremes. They live where temperatures are neither too high nor too low —where pressure is neither too great nor too little— where rainfall is neither too heavy nor too light. But some animals have developed functional adaptations that enable them to live in the extremes. And so we find animals living in every imaginable spot on earth.

Behavioral Adaptations

The sun rises over a lake in East Africa. Male tilapia fish each guard a small area, or territory, some 18 inches around. If a male enters another's territory, the defender opens his mouth wide. The invader either responds with the same threat or retreats. He is chased if he does not leave voluntarily.

A kangaroo rat, which is so-named because it hops around on its long hind legs, stores the seeds it needs for food and a water source in pouches in its cheeks.

However, if a female should enter a male's territory, no such threat is made. The male behaves very differently to attract a female. With his mouth kept closed, he turns to the side to show off his brilliant colors. If his courtship is successful, the two fish mate over a special depression the male has made in the sand for the eggs. During mating, the males in neighboring territories do not intrude.

The female picks up the fertilized eggs in her mouth and goes off with them. She will keep them in her mouth until they hatch. The males continue to defend their territories and mate with females until about 11 a.m. Then all the tilapia, including males who moments before were threatening one another, leave this area of the lake. They swim off together to an area where algae is plentiful to eat.

The afternoon is a lazy time. The fish move about among themselves and nibble the algae. They become excited only if a predator such as a pelican comes along.

But the next morning, the territorial and mating behavior begins again. The males are back in their territories, threatening other males and trying to attract females.

An animal behaves when it reacts to a change in its environment. This may be a change in its external environment—for example, when the male tilapia sees the female and shifts from aggressive to mating behavior. Or it may be a change in the internal environment—for example, the chemical changes in the female's body that prepares her for egg laying.

Although there are many different types of behavioral adaptations, they can be grouped into nine categories, as follows:

Eating behavior is any behavior connected with getting and eating food. The giraffe stands up straight so it can feed in the treetops. Its favorite food is the thorn acacia, a plant covered with sharp spines. But the giraffe works its long tongue between the spines and reaches the leaves.

Very different is the eating behavior of an alligator. It waits quietly in a river, most of its body submerged in water. When it spots prey, such as a bird or a land mammal, it quickly grabs the victim, pulls it into the water, and drowns it.

A giraffe stretches high into leafy trees for food. During the dry season, when the ground is nearly bare of vegetation, the giraffe can still find food.

As an **alligator** grows, it seeks ever larger animals as its prey.

Shelter-seeking behavior is any behavior connected with looking for or building a home. A bear searches for a cave in which to spend the winter months. Prairie dogs build complex underground burrows, complete with listening rooms and toilets. A barn swallow builds a nest of mud and straw under the roof of a barn, then lines it with chicken feathers.

Shelter-seeking behavior also includes behavior designed to protect an animal against poor weather conditions. A tree squirrel, for example, uses its tail to protect itself from the weather. If it rains, the tail is held upward and spread wide like an umbrella. At midday, when the sun is hot, the squirrel uses its tail in a similar way to shade its head and back from the sun. On a cool night, the squirrel uses its tail as a blanket. It curls up in its nest, then spreads its tail over its body.

Some animals react to predators and other aggressors by pretending they are dead. The hognose snake—so named because its snout looks like that of a pig—does this. If an enemy approaches, the snake often first reacts in a way that might scare the intruder. It flattens its head, inhales lots of air so that its body puffs up, and hisses. If this doesn't frighten off the intruder, the snake may roll over onto its back. For a moment or two, it writhes back and forth, as if in agony. Its mouth is open, and its tongue drags on the ground. Then it is still. It very convincingly looks dead—unless it is turned over onto its belly again. Finding itself right-side up, the snake immediately turns over onto its back again.

Mimicry is sometimes a type of defensive behavior. The bittern, a bird with striped and spotted feathers that lives in marshes, can behave as if it is a

A tree squirrel rests on a branch with its bushy tail spread over its body like a blanket.

A hognose snake that has rolled onto its back and looks dead may fool a predator.

Aggressive and defensive behavior is any behavior connected with attack or protective actions between animals. Territorial behavior, such as that between the male tilapias, is an example. So is fighting to determine the leader in a group. When two animals of the same type fight each other, care usually is taken to avoid serious physical injury. For example, when a male oryx antelope fights another male oryx, the two animals use only the upper parts of their horns and direct them only against the opponent's horns. They never attack each other's flanks. But when a male oryx antelope fights off an attacking lion, he tries to gouge the lion's belly with his long, swordlike horns.

reed. It stands very straight and points its bill almost straight up. The killdeer, a ground-nesting bird, will pretend it is injured if a predator threatens its nest. Dragging a wing on the ground, it gradually moves away from the nest. The predator follows, but as it closes in for the kill, its "wounded" victim flies away.

Reproductive behavior is any behavior related to reproduction. This includes finding mates, courtship, and mating. The male tilapia's preparation of a breeding depression and his display of bright colors are examples of reproductive behavior.

Among the more curious reproductive be-

A **bittern** standing very still among the marsh reeds might not be seen by a passing predator.

A **killdeer** may pretend it is injured to draw a predator's attention away from its nestlings.

haviors are those timed to coincide with the phase of the moon and the stages of the tide. For example, in spring and summer, when the moon is new and the tides are high, the male palolo worm *Palola viridis* leaves his protective shelter. He swims rapidly through the water, shedding sperm as he goes. The female follows the male within a short time, releasing her eggs.

Care-giving behavior is any behavior by a parent that is directed toward the care of its offspring. Care-giving behavior begins at the time of egg laying and continues until the young animals are able to take care of themselves. Some animals, particularly the simpler invertebrates, do not provide any care at all for their young. At the other end of the scale are mammals, which provide a great deal of care. For example, a mother koala provides milk for its offspring, protects it, carries it about, and helps it learn how to climb.

A **koala** spends 5 to 6 months in its mother's pouch and then about 6 months clinging to her back. It won't be independent for several years.

Baby robins have enormous appetites. They keep both their parents busy from dawn to dusk bringing them worms, snails, insect larvae, and fruit.

Eliminative behavior is the way in which animals keep themselves and their homes free of body wastes. A cat digs a hole and buries its urine and feces. A dog will eliminate its wastes away from its own territory. A young hawk flips its tail at the same time that it excretes fecal material. This tosses the wastes out of the nest. As with other kinds of behavior, eliminative behavior is not seen in all animals. Some monkeys don't have such behavior—it isn't necessary when you spend all your life on tree limbs far above the ground.

Imitative behavior is any behavior in which members of a group do the same thing. Canada geese form a V as they fly. Herring stay together in large groups called schools. Buffalo gather in herds.

An interesting experiment showed that a desire to be part of the group may affect other behavior. A chick that had finished eating was placed with a group of chicks that had just begun to eat. Moments before, it had shown no interest in more food. Now, however, it began to eat again. Another chick, one that had not eaten, was placed in a group of chicks that had already eaten. Although it was hungry, it did not start to eat until quite some time had passed.

Investigative behavior is any behavior in which an animal confronted with an unfamiliar object or placed in an unfamiliar environment explores the new situation. A monkey will pick up a strange object, turn it around, smell it, and perhaps even taste it. When a cat or a dog enters a house for the first time, it moves from room to room, sniffing everything.

An animal's behavior, as unique as it may be, is related to its structural and functional adaptations. A male tilapia couldn't display his bright colors if he didn't have them. A crocodile couldn't capture the prey it feeds on if it didn't have sharp teeth and powerful jaws. An oryx antelope probably wouldn't challenge a lion if the antelope didn't have long, sharp horns. You wouldn't be reading these words if you didn't have two highly developed eyes and a brain capable of interpreting what the eyes see. All three types of adaptations for survival—structural, functional, and behavioral—combine to create the total picture of each and every animal.

Care-seeking behavior is any behavior that says "I want" or "I need" something. Usually, this behavior is seen in the young and is directed toward their parents. A baby robin opens its mouth wide as it begs for food. A hungry baby heron begs for food by grasping its parent's bill. This stimulates the parent to bring up food it has partly eaten and put it into the young bird's mouth.

Among some animals, care-seeking behavior can occur between two adults. Monkeys of various species will invite other members of their troop to groom them. The groomer will grip the other monkey's fur and slowly draw his hands through the fur. With his teeth he will remove dandruff and other objects. He'll also use his teeth to untangle matted fur. The crested bare-faced tamarin does an even more thorough job. A groomer will stick his long tongue into the other monkey's mouth and clean out debris.

Crab-eating macaques of the Philippines and Malaysia spend much time grooming each other. This behavior is more of a social gesture—assuring each other of their peaceful relationship—than one of actual cleaning.

Staying Alive

Getting food is just one of the basic needs every animal must fulfill in order to stay alive. This chapter looks at specific examples of some of the basic ways animals manage to stay alive:

Lions depend on the element of surprise to catch zebras and other prey.

Rabbits draw upon their keenly developed senses of hearing, sight, and smell to protect themselves from their more powerful enemies.

The squid uses both physical and chemical weapons to help it catch prey and fight off enemies.

The cecropia (si-CROH-pee-a) moth goes through four very different life stages. When it is young, it must eat constantly. As an adult, it does not eat at all. Its only objective as an adult is to mate and produce the next generation.

Weaver birds build intricate, delicate nests to shelter their young and themselves.

Canada geese migrate in order to maintain an adequate food supply and to find the best breeding grounds.

Each of the different animals discussed in this chapter has responded in a different way to basic needs that must be fulfilled in order to stay alive. There are nearly as many unique adaptations to the struggle for life as there are unique animals. And these unique adaptations are apparent in even the smallest and simplest animals.

A stagnant puddle may appear to be lifeless. But take a sample of the water, put a drop on a glass slide, and view it through a microscope. Chances are you will see all sorts of creatures milling about. Some, most likely, will be one-celled animals called paramecia (pehr-a-ME-see-a) (singular: paramecium).

Paramecia can move very quickly. They may move two or three millimeters a second and keep up this speed for hours at a time. A tiny paramecium moving at two or three millimeters a second is like a car traveling at a speed of 100 miles per hour. Moving at such a speed requires a lot of energy. A car gets its energy from gasoline. A paramecium, like all animals, gets its energy from the food it eats. Paramecia mainly feed on bacteria—and they eat a lot of

A honeybee gathers nectar from a flower to make honey. At the same time, pollen collects on stiff hairs on its hind legs.

41

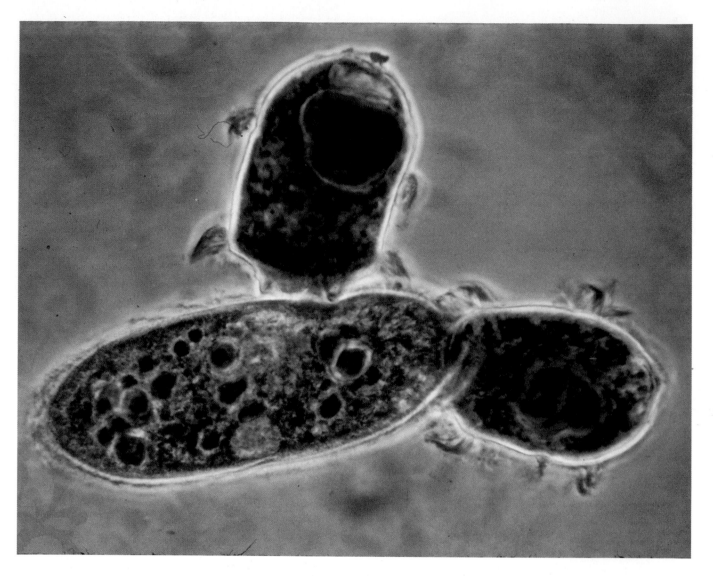

bacteria, perhaps as many as 1,500 bacteria an hour.

A paramecium's main enemy is another one-celled animal, *Didinium nasutum*. This creature, sometimes called the water bear, feeds almost solely on paramecia. It has a long snoutlike structure called a proboscis (pro-BOS-iss) with which it makes jabbing movements as it swims through the water. When its proboscis touches a paramecium, the didinium shoots out venomous hairlike structures called trichocysts (TRIK-a-sists). The trichocysts penetrate the body of the paramecium and cripple it. The paramecium also has trichocysts—it shoots hundreds of them into its attacker. But the didinium is not harmed by the paramecium's weapons.

The didinium uses its trichocysts to hold the paramecium close. Its proboscis then expands enormously, enabling the didinium to swallow the paramecium. A didinium can swallow a paramecium that is twice as big as it is. Moreover, it has a huge appetite. It may eat ten or more paramecia in a day.

Two Didinium nasutum attack a paramecium. A didinium will try to pierce and eat everything in its path—even another didinium.

The paramecia not only provide food for the didinium but they also provide a chemical needed by the didinium to digest the food.

A colony of paramecia doesn't stand a chance against the didinia. However, if the didinia ate all the paramecia, there would be no more food for them and they would starve. The didinia have an excellent adaptation to prevent them from eating up all of their food source. When the paramecium population is low, each didinium forms a dry shell, or cyst, around itself. This is a resting stage. The didinia remain in this state until the paramecium population has rebuilt itself. Then the didinia emerge from their cysts and renew their slaughter. How the didinia know that the paramecia are again plentiful is one of the mysteries that scientists still must solve.

Hunters of the African Plain

As the sun begins to set on the African plain, a herd of zebra quietly graze. Nearby, hidden by tall grass and a clump of bushes, are a group of lions. The lions move slowly, ready to freeze into immobility whenever the zebras look their way.

Gradually, the lions spread out into a wide arc. Then, suddenly, they rush at the zebras. The alarmed zebras race off across the plain. One zebra, less alert than the others or too old to move quickly, does not escape. A lion leaps onto the zebra's back and digs her claws deep into the flesh. She pulls the zebra down.

Other lions rush to help with the killing. In a few minutes, the zebra is dead. One of the lions arches its back and gives a triumphant roar that can be heard for miles. Then all is quiet. As night falls the loudest sounds are the growls and snarls made by the contented eaters.

More often than not, lions do not succeed in catching their prey. It takes a great deal of skill—and a bit of luck—to bring down a zebra or an antelope or a wildebeest.

A lion is built for power, not for speed. Its top speed is about 35 miles per hour. This is slower than the speed at which zebras and most other prey can move. Also, the lion cannot keep up this speed for long. If it doesn't catch its intended victim right away, it gives up. It does not pursue the animal.

To be successful, the lion has to surprise its prey. It tries to get very close to an animal before it attacks. If the lion can get within 100 feet of the animal, it usually can catch it. The prey, however, knows this. They have learned how close to a lion they can be without fearing an attack. And so it is not unusual to see a group of lions and, perhaps 120 feet away, a group of zebras, or antelopes. Each group pretends disinterest in the other but, in reality, is very aware of the distance between them.

In the daytime, the lion's tawny color helps to hide it, for this color blends in with the background. Also, a lion can crouch very low against the ground so that it is nearly invisible. But most of the lion's hunting is done at night, when darkness helps to hide its movements from the zebras and other grazing animals.

The grazers have several adaptations, in addition to speed, that protect them. They have a keen sense of hearing. Many a lion is foiled because the grazers hear it rustling in the grass. The grazers also have an excellent sense of smell. Lions do not take into account the direction of the wind. If they move

An unsuspecting lone **zebra** continues to graze, not realizing that it is being stalked by a **lioness** crouching in the grass. Will it see the lioness in time to turn and flee?

with the wind, the prey will detect their presence while they are still several hundred feet away.

In addition, each type of prey has its own distinctive behavior patterns. The lions must learn these differences and act accordingly. For instance, zebras may stop and defend themselves against an attack. They can deliver very powerful kicks and have been known to drive off attacking lions. A herd of impalas (a medium-sized antelope) will explode into a dozen different directions, with each animal running off in a series of high, twisting leaps. Reedbucks, dik-diks, and duikers (DIE-curz) (three other types of antelopes) may swiftly run for cover, then stand perfectly still until the lions give up looking for them.

Because its prey are so skilled, and because prey may be scarce, a lion may go for a week without catching an animal. But when food is available, the lion stuffs itself. It is not unusual for a lion to eat 50 pounds of meat at one time. After such a meal, the lion will settle down in the grass for a long nap. When food is easy to obtain, a lion will spend about 21 hours of the day sleeping and resting. But when food is scarce, the lion has little time for resting.

A lion will eat almost any animal—if it can catch it. Lions that hunt together may bring down giraffes, buffaloes, and other large animals. A lion hunting by itself will chase smaller game, such as gazelles. It will go after rabbits, mice, and rats. It may attack a porcupine, though the quills of the porcupine can leave nasty wounds on the lion's face or paws. Crocodiles, snakes, even termites and other insects may fall prey to a lion. So may fish. With a swipe of its paw, a lion can catch fish swimming in shallow water. In areas settled by people, lions may kill cattle and other domesticated animals. They also may attack and kill people, though this is not common. Nor is it common for lions to attack the African elephant. This animal's tusks and large size are excellent protective devices. So is the close-knit social structure of the elephant herd.

Often, lions scavenge for food. That is, they eat animals that died naturally or that were killed by other animals. The lions will watch the sky for vultures. They have learned that these birds gather where meat is to be found. They also listen for the laughing sounds of hyenas, then go and chase the hyenas away from the food. But it can work the other way, too. Sometimes hyenas chase lions away from the remains of the lions' kill.

Some lions hunt alone or in pairs. But most lions live and hunt in groups. These groups are called prides. A pride may consist of as many as 35 lions. Such large prides are found in areas where there is a lot of game. In areas where game is scarce, prides are much smaller, containing perhaps only half-a-dozen members.

Basically, a pride is a family group. A typical larger pride may contain 2 males, 13 females, and 20

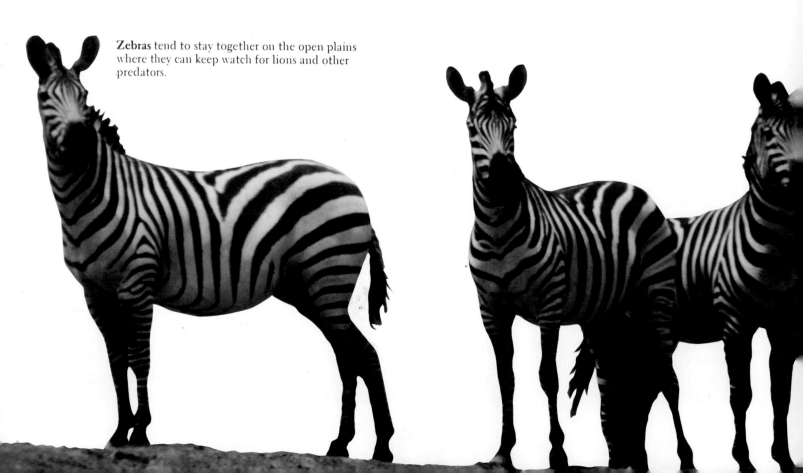

Zebras tend to stay together on the open plains where they can keep watch for lions and other predators.

Lions tear into the flesh of their prey with their large, pointed front teeth—the canines. All 30 of their teeth are sharply pointed. They have no flat teeth (molars) with which to chew their food. They must swallow their food in large chunks.

cubs. The females usually are all related to one another. There may be three or even four generations of lionesses, plus their cubs. The males in the pride are temporary members. They are not related. The males may stay only a few weeks or they may remain with the group for several years. However, sooner or later they leave, perhaps after being chased out by other males.

Male cubs, sons of lionesses in the pride, are driven out of the group when they are about 3 years old. They wander through the plains alone or in twos or threes. When they are about 5 years old and fully grown, they may join a pride whose males have died, or they may force out a male lion from a pride and take over his group. Some males remain loners, never becoming part of a pride. If such a male comes upon a pride feasting on a kill, it may try to chase the pride off. If successful, it will settle down to fill its stomach.

Within a pride, it is the females who do most of the hunting. Often the lionesses cooperate with one another to catch an animal. The male members of the pride also have important roles to play. First, they stay with the cubs while the lionesses hunt,

thereby protecting the youngsters. Second, the males maintain and defend the pride's territory—the area occupied by the pride. By keeping out other lions, as well as other predators, the males provide the females with a safe place to raise cubs. A study of two neighboring prides showed how important this role of the male is. One pride had only one male. In a two-year period 26 cubs were born but only 2 survived. The other pride had 3 males. In the same two-year period 20 cubs were born, 12 of which survived.

How an intruder into a pride's territory is greeted may depend on whether it is a male or a female. If a strange lioness wanders by, a male member of the pride may greet her warmly and try to mate with her. But the lionesses of the pride will drive her off. Lionesses may welcome a strange male, but the pride's males will chase him until he's well away from the pride.

Among themselves, pride members are affectionate. They nuzzle one another when they meet, sleep together, and playfully wrestle. Only when they eat are they hostile to one another. The males usually get first choice of the meat. When it is the turn of the lionesses, they may shove their cubs away from the fallen prey. The cubs only get to eat the leftovers. Lions may cooperate in hunting and other activities, but when it comes to eating, it's every lion for itself.

A Rabbit's Senses

A European hare is about 28 inches long. Its ears are about 5 inches long. In other words, its body is about 5½ times as long as its ears. Measure your ears and height. You will find that your body is more than 30 times as long as your ears.

Rabbits and hares are much more dependent on sounds than are people. At night, as they search for food in fields and meadows, they prick up their ears at the slightest sound. Quickly they locate the direction from which the sound is coming. If they judge it to be a threat, they run toward home. If the sound is one they recognize as harmless—the rustling of leaves in the breeze, the chirping of crickets, the singing of a nightingale—they return to their grazing.

Having two ears, one on either side of the head, helps a rabbit locate the source of a sound. It can tell if the sound is coming from the right or from the left. A sound coming from the right is louder in the right ear than in the left ear. This is because the head creates a "shadow" between the sound and the left ear. The sound also reaches the right ear before it reaches the left ear because the right ear is nearer to the sources of the sound.

Sounds coming from the front and the back affect both ears the same way. To tell from which of these two directions the sound is coming, a rabbit need not turn its head. Special muscles enable rabbits to just turn their ears. As soon as a rabbit hears an unusual sound, its ears will react. The ears move this way and that, until they locate the source of the sound. You have these same muscles in your ears, but they are not well developed.

European rabbits live in burrows, hidden from enemies such as hawks and weasels. Their fine sense of hearing is one of the rabbits' main weapons of defense against their enemies.

A rabbit does not depend solely on its sense of hearing to detect danger. Sight also is important. The rabbit's large eyes are located on the sides of its head. Because of this, the rabbit can see to the front, to the sides, to some distance behind, and even overhead without turning its head. Unlike human eyes, which focus on the same spot, a rabbit's eyes usually focus on two different views. If one view seems more important, the rabbit's brain concentrates on that image and ignores the other.

There is one important visual adaptation that rabbits do not have. A rabbit does not see colors. Everything in its world exists in tones of black, gray and white. This presents problems unknown to an animal that has color vision. Suppose, for instance, that a rabbit sees a hawk land on a branch. Knowing that the hawk is an enemy, the rabbit freezes. It stays very still, hoping to avoid the notice of the hawk. It watches the hawk closely. If, however, the hawk also remains still, the rabbit gradually relaxes. Perhaps it looks elsewhere. Once it does this, it loses track of the bird. If it looks back toward the hawk, the bird will have blended into the surrounding trees and bushes, all of which, to the rabbit, are black and white. Unless the hawk moves, the rabbit will be unable to locate it. It may forget about the hawk and hop toward another patch of grass—an error that could cost it its life.

The third sense that provides a rabbit with needed information about friends and enemies is the sense of smell. The twitching of its sensitive nose soon tells it who is nearby.

The sense of smell plays a particularly important role in identifying other rabbits. A male rabbit marks his territory by laying down a special fluid. This fluid is secreted from glands on his chin. Using one of his hind legs, he scratches the glands, thereby releasing the fluid. Other rabbits smell this and learn that they are intruding.

Sometimes a male will put his scent on youngsters and females in his group. He does this by rubbing his chin over the other animals. This reduces the chance of fighting among members of a group. It also enables a rabbit to quickly identify a stranger—any rabbit that does not share the family scent.

When a female is ready to mate, she gives off a special scent. Males smell this scent and follow it until they find the female.

The rabbit's ears, eyes, and nose are constantly at work, feeding information about the environment to the rabbit's brain. The way the rabbit behaves tells a great deal about the information being picked up by these important sensory organs.

The European hare has long, sensitive ears. By moving them from side to side, it can quickly locate the source of a sound. The large ears also serve a second function. They enable the animal to lose excess heat. If the hare is too hot, blood vessels in its ears enlarge. Heat passes out of the blood and skin into the air.

The Weapons of a Squid

"Schooner Sunk by a Squid" reported the headline in the *Mystic* (Connecticut) *Press.* The newspaper account seemed almost matter-of-fact. It sounded as if such incidents happened all the time.

The story, dated July 31, 1874, told how the 150-ton schooner *Pearl* was sunk by a giant squid on May 10th of that year. "The sinking was witnessed and reported by passenger steamer *Strathowen*. Passengers first noted a large brownish mass lying on the surface between the steamer and the schooner, which was becalmed two or three miles away. Someone on the schooner fired a rifle at the object and it began to move toward the schooner and squeezed on board between the fore and mainmast, pulling the vessel over and sinking it. Its body was as thick as the schooner and about half as long, with a train that appeared to be 100 feet long. The steamer put out boats and picked up five of the crew swimming in the water. The other members of the crew were crushed between the mast and one of the creature's tentacles, which were as thick as a barrel."

Other, similar tales were told by many fishermen and whalers of the 1800s. Captain Haley, who sailed on the whaling ship *Charles W. Morgan*, told of seeing a 300-foot-long squid. Swimming alongside it, said Haley, were two 150-foot-long squids.

The restored whaling ship *Charles W. Morgan* is now docked in Mystic Seaport in Connecticut.

Were these stories true? Do such monstrous squids swim in the oceans of the world? The evidence indicates that the answer to these questions is "no." No 300-foot-, or even 100-foot-long squid has ever been captured or photographed.

This is not to say that some squids aren't very large. The giant squid is the largest invertebrate (animal without a backbone) known to us. Its length may exceed 50 feet—about nine times the height of an average person. Combine this huge size with all the squid's well-developed weapons and it can indeed be a frightening enemy.

About 375 different species of squids live in the oceans of the world. Some species live in shallow waters. Others may be found at depths of 5,000 feet or more. They range in size from the largest, the giant squid, down to species that are less than an inch long.

Squids are mollusks. Other mollusks are snails; slugs; shellfish such as oysters, clams, and scallops; and the octopus and the nautilus. Together with the octopus and the nautilus the squid belongs to the group of mollusks called cephalopods (SEF-a-la-pods.) This name comes from two Greek words meaning "head" and "foot." "Head-foot" is an appropriate name, for a quick glimpse gives the impression that the animal is made only of these two parts. Actually, of course, it has a complete body. The streamlined body shaped like a torpedo is covered by a muscular tissue called the mantle. Two large fins are attached to the back part of the body. At the front end of the body is the well-developed head. The foot, which has been modified into a ring of long arms, is attached to the front end of the head.

A squid is both predator and prey. It feeds on other animals. In turn, it is eaten by other predators. To catch its victims and to avoid capture itself, the squid uses a variety of weapons.

Of major importance, both for offense and defense, are the squid's muscular arms. A squid has ten arms—two more than its relative the octopus. In some species of squid, all the arms are the same length. In other species, one pair—called the tentacles—are longer than the others. This is true for the giant squids. One giant squid caught off the coast of New Zealand had a body length of 26 feet and tentacles that were 46 feet long!

The arms of a squid are covered with rows of suckers, with each sucker attached to the arm by a short muscular stalk. The size of the suckers varies greatly. In some species, the suckers are 2 to 3 inches in diameter. In others they are less than 1/100th of an inch across.

A squid's tentacles are covered with suckers having teethlike projections that attach to prey.

In most species, the suckers are rimmed with hooks or teeth. The common American squid, for example, has two rows of suckers running the length of each of its eight shorter arms. The two tentacle-arms have enlarged clublike ends, each of which has four or more rows of suckers.

The squid can shoot out its tentacles with great speed. As soon as the tentacles make contact, the suckers are attached to the prey. The tentacles then draw the prey inward. Some of the other arms also attach their suckers to the prey and help move it toward the mouth. Then the arms hold the prey while the squid tears off pieces of the victim.

To help kill its prey, the squid produces a powerful poison called cephalotoxin (SEF-a-low-tox-in). This is present in the squid's saliva.

The round mouth of the squid has two powerful jaws. These look somewhat like the beak of a parrot except that they curve inward. The upper jaw pushes down between the cutting edges of the lower jaw with tremendous force. Fish skulls and crab skeletons are easily crushed by this action. So is fishing equipment. Fishermen off the coast of Peru tell of the powerful jaws of the Humboldt Current squid, an aggressive creature that may be 12 feet long and

weigh 300 pounds. According to the fishermen, the bite of the Humboldt Current squid causes more damage to their equipment—including steel boat hooks—than does the bite of a shark. It's no wonder that the fishermen are afraid of this creature. Said one fisherman, "These are not fish, or animal, but demon."

Being able to make a quick escape is another weapon in a squid's arsenal. When swimming slowly, the squid uses its fins. But when speed is necessary, the squid moves by jet propulsion. Water enters the mantle cavity—the space between the mantle and the body. The mantle then is contracted and the water is ejected forcibly through a funnel, or siphon.

The opening of the siphon is on the underside of the body, just behind the arms. The water is ejected toward the arms, so the squid moves in the opposite direction—that is, backward. To decrease water resistance, some squids flatten their fins close to the body as they shoot backward.

Many squids are not only fast swimmers but very powerful swimmers as well. The strongest

A giant squid is a terrifying sight indeed as it races through the water in search of a meal. The squid swims backward by filling folds in its body walls with water and forcing the water through a tube beneath its head.

49

swimmers probably are the sea arrows, or flying squids. They attain speeds of more than 30 miles per hour and, in the process, build up enough momentum to leap into the air. Some may leap more than 10 feet above the surface of the sea and "fly" 30 feet before landing on the water. A ship off the coast of Brazil got in the path of a school of flying squids. Hundreds landed on the ship's deck, which was 12 feet above the water's surface.

Squids eject a cloud of dark brown ink when they are trying to escape from a pursuer. The cloud temporarily hides the movements of the squid. It also seems to confuse the pursuer, perhaps by deadening the animal's sense of smell.

The squid's ink is produced by special glands in an organ called the ink sac. The ink passes out of the body through an opening near the opening of the siphon. The ink is very strong. A few drops are enough to cloud a large volume of water. The ink also is long-lasting. Some dried ink taken from fossilized squids more than 100 million years old was mixed with water. It made a very fine writing ink!

Some deep-sea squids have pouches filled with luminescent (light-producing) bacteria. When the ink is released, so are some of the bacteria. The result is a glaring cloud of light.

Besides having pouches filled with luminescent bacteria, many types of squid have their own light-producing organs. When these squids light up they look like underwater Christmas trees. The light produced may prevent predators from below seeing a shadow of the squid swimming near the surface during daylight.

The number of light-producing organs, their type, and their location vary from species to species. The jeweled squid has 22 light-producing organs of at least 10 different types. Ruby red lights are located on the front of its belly. A string of pearly white lights run along the side of the body. At the back end of the animal is a cluster of white lights surrounding one sky blue light. And in the center of each eye there are brilliant blue lights.

Squids have the ability to quickly change color. This can be used for camouflage, to hide the squid from prey or predators. For instance, the short-finned squid is typically covered with red and brown spots. But when moving through a school of mackerel it turns a pale, almost translucent color.

The change of color may also be an emotional reaction. A squid at rest may be a pale, neutral color. But if the squid sees something that frightens, angers, or excites it, it may turn bright red.

The colors, or pigments, are contained in special

The California market squid (*Loligo opalescens*) is a favorite food in the Far East.

A squid's eyes do not always match. One may be suited to dark depths, the other to surface light.

cells called chromatophores (croh-MAT-a-fors), which are scattered over the squid's body. Many different pigments may be contained in the chromatophores. Thus a squid may be able to change from one color to another to still another, until it has turned all the colors of the rainbow. Sometimes, each color is sharply defined. At other times or in other species, the colors blend in with one another.

All of the squid's weapons would be of little value if they were not used efficiently. The squid can respond quickly to stimuli because of its highly developed eyes and brain.

The squid's eyes are more like human eyes than those of almost any other animal. They can see color and great detail. In some species the eyes can be moved in and out like a telescope, thereby making it easier to focus on an object. The eyes also are very large. Those of the giant squid may be almost 16 inches in diameter!

The brain of the squid is large and complex. Between it and the muscles of the mantle and arms run many giant nerve fibers. These quickly carry messages from the brain to the muscles, enabling the squid to react quickly to prey or predator.

With such an arsenal of highly developed structures, squids do not have many friends. A swarm of sea arrows can terrorize a school of mackerel or herring. Squids also feed on squids smaller than themselves, and even on the young of their own species.

Sharks, rays, and toothed whales are the main predators of squids. Even the giant squid is not free from attacks by these animals. In fact, a battle

between a giant squid and a sperm whale is one that the squid rarely wins. It is, however, a ferocious battle. Though the whale wins, it does not escape unharmed. Many a whale later caught by people was covered with large circular scars where squid suckers had once gripped hard.

Do squids attack people? Will they attack you if you go swimming or sailing in the ocean?

On March 25, 1941, during World War II, the troopship *Britannia* was sunk by a German raider in the Atlantic Ocean. Twelve men who escaped from the sinking ship clung to a small raft. At night, one sailor was pulled under and killed by a squid.

Such stories—at least ones supported by evidence or by reliable eyewitnesses—are rare. Certainly there is little if any danger if you swim in coastal waters during the day. Almost all of the larger squids are night creatures that spend the daylight hours resting in deep waters.

However, if a giant squid is spotted in the area, it's best to keep out of the water. And don't go for a midnight swim off the coast of Peru when the Humboldt Current squids are out looking for a meal.

Some Types of Squid

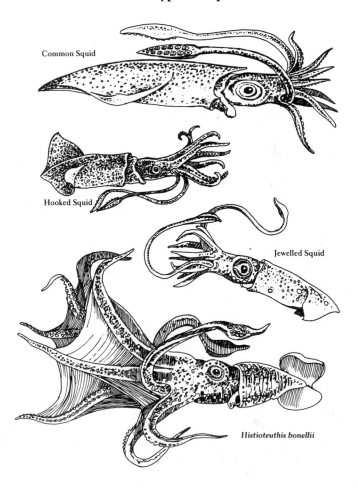

Common Squid

Hooked Squid

Jewelled Squid

Histioteuthis bonellii

A cecropia moth deposits her eggs on a twig.

Newly hatched cecropia caterpillars emerge from their eggs and immediately begin to eat.

From Caterpillar to Moth

When it is young it eats constantly. When it is an adult it does not eat at all.

When it is young it crawls about on tiny legs. When it is an adult it flies through the air.

When it is young it is colorful but ugly. As an adult it is colorful . . . and beautiful.

The cecropia (si-CROH-pee-a) moth, which lives in the eastern United States, has one of the most wondrous life cycles of the animal world. During its life, its form completely changes. When it is young it is a caterpillar. Then it goes through a resting stage during which its body changes completely. When it emerges from the resting stage, it is a moth.

The life cycle begins in late spring or early summer, when a female cecropia moth lays her eggs. The large oval eggs are a creamy color, with reddish-brown spots. They are laid in scattered patches on a branch or leaf of a plant that will later serve as a source of food for the young insects.

The eggs hatch in about ten days. Out of each comes a tiny caterpillar. It is black and covered with short bristles. As it grows, its color will change to a green that blends in with the leaves on which it feeds. Down its back will be two rows of yellow knobs. Near its head will be four large red knobs. The knobs, which are covered with bristles, make the caterpillar unattractive to birds and other predators.

The skin of a caterpillar is like a hard outer shell. Unlike human skin, it does not grow. If the caterpillar is to grow, it must replace the skin with a larger skin. Within a week after its birth, the caterpillar sheds its skin (molts) for the first time. The cecropia caterpillar will molt four times during its life. Each time, a new skin forms under the old skin. The old skin then cracks. The caterpillar expands and contracts its muscles until it has wiggled out of the old skin. It immediately takes in a lot of air, making its body swell as much as possible while the new skin is still soft and elastic. In a few hours, when the skin has hardened, the outer limits of growth are set.

Molting is controlled by a chemical known as the juvenile hormone. This hormone regulates growth, ensuring that the caterpillar has the proper number of molts and reaches normal size before it changes into an adult. Once development is complete, the juvenile hormone is no longer needed and the body stops producing it.

Some interesting experiments have been done to show what happens if the release of juvenile hormone is tampered with. If the gland that produces the juvenile hormone is removed, the caterpillar stops growing and turns into a very tiny adult—a dwarf. In contrast, if the gland from a young caterpillar is transplanted into a caterpillar that has almost completed its growth, it will continue to grow and molt. After making its last molt, it turns into an abnormally large moth—a giant.

The well-developed mouth parts of the cecropia caterpillar are designed for chewing and biting. It feeds on the leaves of many broad-leafed trees. It keeps eating until it is a fat wormlike creature about four inches long. It reaches this full size by early autumn and then seeks out a suitable twig on which to change into an adult. It then spins a cocoon of silk around itself. The cocoon will protect the insect during the cold winter months and during the change from caterpillar to moth.

The silk is produced by organs that actually are modified salivary glands. They consist of long tubes that stretch along the underside of the caterpillar,

A mature cecropia caterpillar spins its cocoon within a leaf to protect it over the winter.

A male cecropia moth lands on a cocoon where the next generation is undergoing metamorphosis.

from its lower jaw to its midsection. The lower jaw contains special muscles that squeeze the silk so that it is secreted as a fine thread.

As the caterpillar secretes the silk, it slowly moves its head back and forth. It firmly attaches the silk to various parts of the twig. Then it shapes the saclike cocoon around its body. Once the outer layer is completed, the caterpillar spins a fine inner lining.

When it has finished the cocoon, the caterpillar undergoes a final molt and enters the resting stage. During this period, which lasts through the winter, the insect doesn't move or feed. However, this stage is essential, as is the exposure to cold temperatures. If the resting stage isn't exposed to temperatures between 37 and 41°F for at least one-and-a-half months, the caterpillar will not change into a moth.

The first warm days of spring trigger the production of a special hormone by the brain. This is carried by the blood to a gland just behind the head, which is stimulated to produce another hormone. These two hormones are responsible for the great changes that now begin to take place in the insect's body. The old tissues of the caterpillar's body are broken down and from them new tissues are built. Long antennae, eyes, and three pairs of long, thin legs develop. Two pairs of wings grow. Reproductive organs, either male or female, are formed.

The change of the body from one form—the caterpillar—to another—the moth—is called metamorphosis. This comes from Greek words meaning "change of form." Many animals undergo metamorphosis during their life cycle, though few make as great a change as do moths and butterflies.

The built-in mechanism that requires a lengthy period of cold followed by a warming trend before the adult begins to form is an important adaptation for the temperate-climate cecropia. It prevents metamorphosis from occurring during the winter, when the adult would not be able to survive. And since metamorphosis is triggered by an external event—warm weather—that affects all resting stages the same way at the same time, all the adult cecropias will emerge from their cocoons at more or less the same time. This ensures that males and females will be able to find each other and mate.

It takes about 21 days for the cecropia adult to fully form. Then the cocoon begins to break. At the head end, there is a valve-like structure. When the moth pushes against it, it opens and the moth pokes its head out. Using its legs, it works its way out of the cocoon.

At first, the cecropia moth is very sluggish. Its wings are folded tightly against its body and are soft and fragile. As the moth clings to the twig, blood begins to flow into the wings, expanding them. When the wings are fully developed the moth spreads them wide, revealing their dramatic pattern. They are reddish-brown and crossed in the middle with a band of white. In the center of each of the four wings is a crescent-shaped white spot and at the outer tip of each forewing is a dark spot.

The cecropia moth has only one function: to reproduce the species. Its mouthparts are so reduced that is unable to eat. Thus no energy is wasted on gathering and digesting food. Rather, the energy needed during this period is provided by fat produced during the caterpillar stage and now stored in the adult's body.

The cecropia moth flies around until it finds a mate. After mating, the female lays her eggs. Her job done, she soon dies. But within the eggs, a new cycle of life is beginning.

Master Nest Builders

In the towns of central and western Africa there are many people who are excellent weavers. But their skills are equalled by another resident of their communities: a small songbird called the village weaver. This bird builds an intricately woven nest that is suspended from the branch of a tree. The village weaver also is a nonstop talker, and its shrill chatter competes with that of people who live nearby.

The village weaver does not live only in human communities. It forms its own villages wherever it can find a large tree, such as a baobab or a silk-cotton tree. It is not unusual to find 100 or more nests cluttered closely together on a single tree.

The village weaver makes its nest from strips of leaves. It may use the leaves of the tree on which it is building the nest. Or it may use certain grasses. Along the lower part of the Niger River, borghu grass is a favorite nesting material. In spring a visitor to the area will see weaver birds flying toward their nesting site with long trailing streamers of borghu grass held in their bills.

Weaver birds often build their nests in human settlements, as in this African village.

Distribution of Weaver Birds

Africa

India

Indochina

Malaysia

Indonesia

Madagascar

Malabo

São Tomé

Gulf of Guinea

The first step in making the nest is to cut the strips of leaf. The bird begins by biting a slit in the leaf blade. This separates the end of the blade into two parts. Next, it gets a firm grip on the end of one part. As it flies off, holding the end in its beak, a long strip is torn from the leaf.

With the first strips it cuts, the village weaver makes a firm ring on the twig that will hold the nest. This is the basic foundation of the nest. Using the ring as a perch, the bird weaves other strips in and out through the ring. First, a roof is built. Then a room that will house the eggs and nestlings is made. A small outer room is added on. Finally, an entrance is built. The result is a strong, compact structure with its opening on the lower side. The opening usually is through a short entrance tube, which hangs downward. The nest is lined with soft plant fibers.

The village weaver is one of about 100 known species of weaver birds. Most of the species are native to Africa south of the Sahara Desert. A few are found on Madagascar and some live in southern Asia. Most of the birds are about 6 inches from the tip of their beak to the end of their tail. Some are even smaller. The giant weaver, which lives on the island of São Tomé in the Gulf of Guinea, is the largest known weaver bird. It is about 8 inches long.

Although all of these birds weave their nests, there is some variety in the design of the nests and in their location. In some species, males and females work together to build their nests. In other species the male builds the nest to attract a female, who may then be responsible for lining the nest.

It is surprising how quickly a weaver bird can complete its home, considering how complex the nest is. For example, one bird began building at 8:30 a.m. By 9:45 he had finished the initial ring. By 1:30 the nesting room was on and by 5:30 that afternoon the structure was almost finished. The following morning the lining was put in and the home was complete.

Some nests, which are more complicated to build, have long entrance tubes. The advantage of a long entrance tube was described by John Hurrell Crook of the University of Bristol in England: "I was observing a colony of Baya weavers above a well in an Indian village when a snake came slithering along a limb. It tried to crawl down to the nest opening by spiraling around the nest tube. But the tube's fine mesh contracted, causing the reptile to slip and plunge into the water below."

The São Tomé weaver, another species found only on the island of São Tomé, is a forest bird that usually builds a round nest with a funnel-like en-

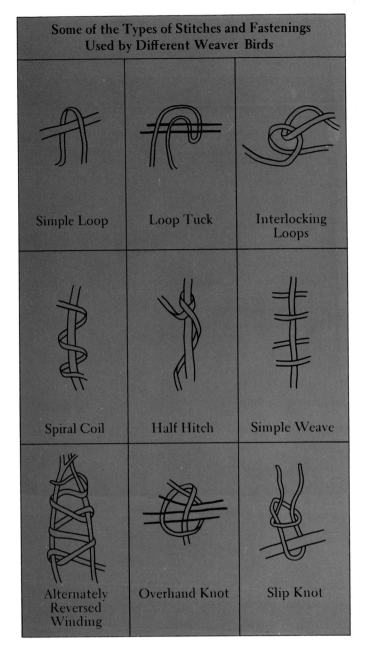

Some of the Types of Stitches and Fastenings Used by Different Weaver Birds

Simple Loop	Loop Tuck	Interlocking Loops
Spiral Coil	Half Hitch	Simple Weave
Alternately Reversed Winding	Overhand Knot	Slip Knot

trance. It uses creeping plants and twigs as building materials and lichens (moss-like plants) for the lining. Some of these birds, however, build communal nests, with individual areas for each family and a common connecting passageway.

In addition to the village weavers, many other species of weaver birds have adapted well to the presence of people. The baya weaver of Asia may build its long, hanging nest on the straw roof of a porch, from telephone wires, or on the coarse blades in a field of sugarcane.

But other species are very shy. The brown-capped weaver, a handsome bird that lives in the mountains of Cameroon, quickly disappears into the treetops when it is alarmed. It often builds its nest on

The **masked weaver** (above) builds its nest high in a tree with an entrance near the bottom.
The **black swamp weaver** makes its nest in tall grass or reeds with an entrance near the top.

acacia trees, which have feathery leaves and many thorns. The nest is attached to the underside of a branch rather than suspended from a ring.

Many weaver birds are polygamous (pa-LIG-a-mus). That is, a male has more than one mate. The male baya weaver usually owns 2 or 3 nests in a colony. When a female accepts and moves into his first nest, he goes on to build other nests to attract other mates. This bird uses grasses or the leaves of rice, sugarcane, or coconut palms for his building material. The nest isn't lined, though he may put blobs of mud on the ceiling. The nest usually is suspended over water—a village well, a pool, or a canal. If one of his nests is rejected by the females, he will cut it down or tear it apart, then start another.

People who share their environment with the weaver birds generally enjoy having the birds around, but sometimes the birds create problems. Weavers are seed-eaters and may invade rice paddies, corn fields, and other farmland, causing much damage. Abandoned nests can also cause problems. During the dry season, these can be a fire hazard. If a fire reaches a tree covered with nests, the attachments between nest and branch are quickly burnt through. If there is a strong wind, the burning nest may then be carried hundreds of feet through the air, landing and starting a fire in another part of the forest, grassland, or village.

Moving with the Seasons

Have you ever looked up in the autumn skies and seen a flock of birds moving in the form of a giant V? What are these birds? Where are they coming from and where are they going?

The birds are Canada geese. They spend the summer in Canada and the northern United States. Then in September and October they begin to fly south. They follow one of four different routes as they head toward their winter homes in the southern United States. If you live along one of these routes, you can see the geese flying in V formation.

The birds fly in a V because it requires less work. The lead bird has the hardest job. It must break the air. This causes upward movements of air to form off the tips of its wings. The following birds ride these updrafts. This is easier than breaking the air. It is very important that the geese stay evenly separated as they fly. Otherwise, the updrafts are not used effectively and flying takes more work.

Sometimes, instead of a V formation, the group forms a long string. But if you look closely, you will see that each bird is flying a little to the side of the bird in front of it, making use of the updrafts.

The geese fly at speeds of 30 to 60 miles per hour. The lead bird may be a male, although it more commonly is a female. As the lead bird tires, it falls back and another bird takes its place.

The four migration routes, or flyways, used by Canada geese and other North American water birds are the Atlantic, Mississippi, Central, and Pacific flyways (see the map). These flyways overlap in places, particularly in Canada, and join in Central America and northern South America. However, any one bird always travels along the same flyway. If it flies along the Atlantic flyway in the first year of its life, it will do so in the following years as well.

Canada geese fly in formation, usually a V, to make the best use of updrafts. When the leader tires, another goose moves forward.

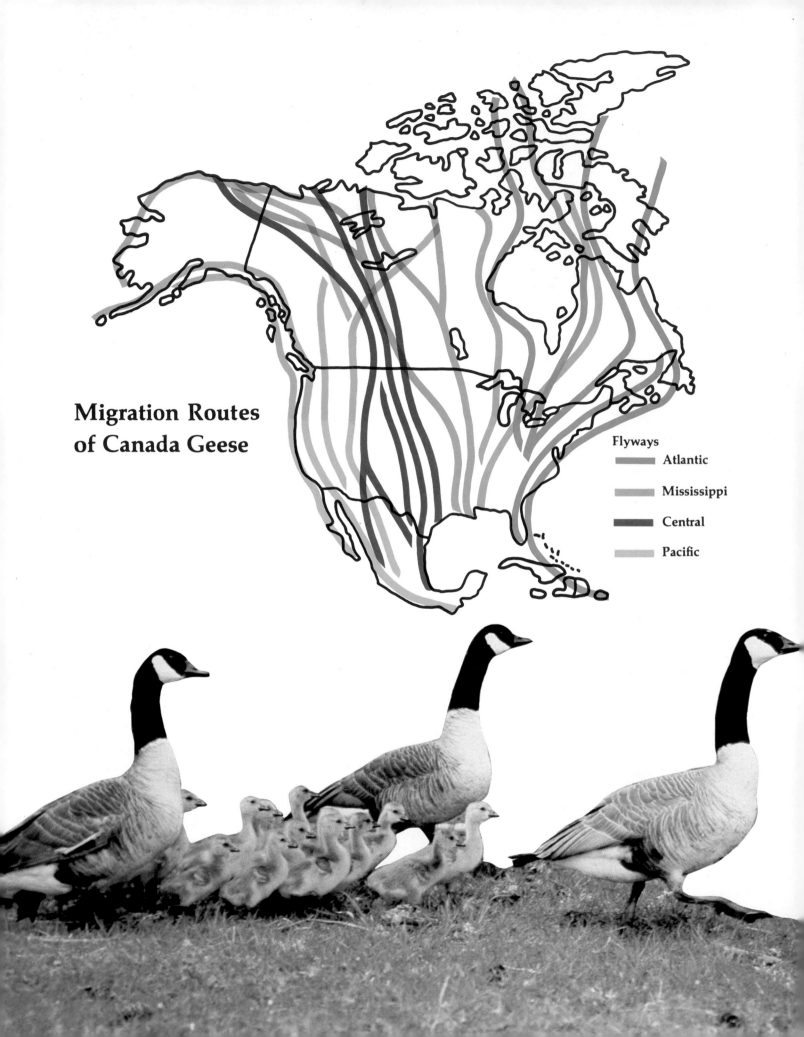

Migration Routes
of Canada Geese

Flyways

Atlantic

Mississippi

Central

Pacific

These **Canada geese** remained near Toronto for the winter. People provided food and shelter.

Wildlife managers and other people interested in preserving wild birds have put their knowledge of the flyways to good use. They have set up refuges along the routes where the birds can feed and rest. Protected areas also have been established in the birds' northern nesting grounds and in the southern areas where they winter.

Canada geese do not travel nonstop. They land for rest periods that may last several hours or several days. The length of such stopovers depends largely on food supplies and on the weather. If the geese find a spot with plenty of food, and if the weather is pleasant, they will stay for a while. Migration also comes to a halt if there is fog, a storm, or heavy winds.

If you live along a flyway, you often will hear Canada geese before seeing them. And if you listen closely, you will realize that the birds' call is not "honk, honk" but "uh-whonk, uh-whonk." This is not the only sound made by Canada geese. Scientists have identified ten different sounds, including hisses, screams, and a snorelike mating call.

All Canada geese belong to the species *Branta canadensis.* There are eight different types, or subspecies. They look very much alike but they are different sizes. The biggest one may weigh 15 pounds and have a wingspan of more than 6 feet. These are the geese that make the honking sound as they migrate. The smaller type weighs about 3 pounds and is more likely to cackle than to honk.

Each autumn about 3 million Canada geese begin the journey south. Only half will reach the winter grounds. Most of the others will be shot by hunters. This sounds cruel, but it is important to the survival of the remaining geese. In the wintering grounds there is enough food for only 1½ million geese. If all the geese arrived, many of them would starve to death.

Canada geese feed on many different types of plants, including grasses, rushes, pondweed, seeds, and berries. A field of young, green wheat or rye is sure to attract them—something a farmer does not appreciate!

In March, the geese begin to fly northward toward their summer homes, where they will nest and raise young. Again, they travel at a leisurely pace. They follow the thaw, not moving onward until temperatures are above the freezing point. Thus they are less likely to be threatened by late winter storms or to find their feeding areas covered with snow.

As people see the V formations moving northward overhead and hear the birds' familiar call, they know that warm weather is coming.

The examples in this chapter have illustrated the variety of ways animals must adapt to their environments in order to stay alive. Nearly all the examples also touched on the topic of the next chapter—the need not only to stay alive but also to reproduce the species, the need to ensure that life will continue for each type of animal.

Continuing Life

Every animal has an overwhelming drive to reproduce, to fill its habitat with more of its kind. This really is the primary purpose of every animal's existence. This chapter looks at ways animals assure the continuance of life for their species. After first observing the reproductive cycle at a small pond, the chapter looks at some simple animals that reproduce without a mate. Next it looks at examples of animals that must find mates in order for life to continue. To assure the continuance of life involves more than just producing offspring. The survival of the offspring, or at least some of them, is just as important. So the next section of this chapter looks at the parental care provided by a number of animals. The final section of the chapter looks at one particular type of parental care–how mammals provide food for their newborn off spring.

During the day, common leopard frogs rest in hiding places along the edges of a small pond. At dusk, the males leave these secluded spots and move into the pond. Each male goes to a calling station. He breathes in large amounts of air, inflating his lungs and puffing up his vocal pouches, which look like two balloons—one on each side of his head. His loud chuckling call, produced by forcibly exhaling air across his vocal chords, resounds across the pond.

The female frogs, their bodies swollen with eggs, may ignore the croaking of a single male frog. But the chorus sung by many males is irresistible. They move toward the males. When the females reach the calling sites, each is grabbed by a male, who puts his arms around her in a tight embrace. The female releases her eggs into the water. At the same time, the male releases sperm that fertilize the eggs.

As many as 6,000 eggs will be laid by the female leopard frog. The eggs, each coated with a protective covering of jelly, form a globe-shaped mass that is attached to vegetation beneath the water's surface. Within each egg, a new leopard frog begins to form. Many never hatch, for they become a meal for a hungry fish or other predator. But a few of the eggs survive, hatch, and so give rise to new leopard frogs after passing through the tadpole stage of development.

As the leopard frogs mate in the water, a similar event is taking place in the air above. A huge swarm

Two butterflies mate in a meadow in Switzerland. The mating may last for up to two hours.

An egg mass laid by a female leopard frog.

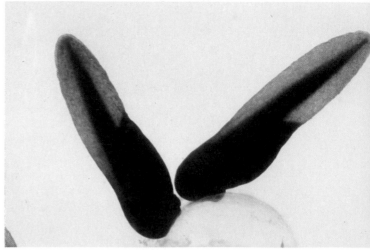

Leopard frog tadpoles just hatched from the eggs.

As a tadpole matures, legs gradually develop.

A mature leopard frog has lost its tadpole tail.

of male mosquitoes forms and moves through the air. The dancing swarm is seen by the female mosquitoes that live around the pond. The females fly to the swarm. A male will be attracted by the buzzing sound made by the wings of a mature female. (Immature females, which have no eggs, produce a lower-pitched buzz that doesn't attract the males.) The male flies over and grabs the female with his legs. They fly off, away from the noisy swarm, to mate.

Later, the female will lay the fertilized eggs on the water near the edge of the pond. She deposits them side by side, forming a raft that floats on the surface. Some of the eggs will be eaten by predators—including baby frogs. Others will hatch in one to three days, giving birth to new mosquitoes.

In the woodlands that surround the pond, other animals may also be mating. A female mouse is attracted to the scent of a male mouse—and vice versa. They mate and three weeks later the female gives birth to a litter of tiny mice. A female deer is courted by a male deer. They mate and seven months later she bears two baby deer. Each animal reproduces its own kind so that life may continue.

The ability to produce offspring of the same kind, or species, is essential if the species is to survive. In fact, the number of individuals produced in a given period—the birth rate—must be at least as great as the number that die—the death rate. If this isn't true, the species will decline in number. It may even become extinct. Many times in the earth's history species have become extinct because they were unable to produce enough offspring.

Reproduction without a Mate

In some lower forms of animals, two parents are not always needed for reproduction. Such reproduction without a mate is called asexual reproduction. The simplest type of asexual reproduction is fission. Many one-celled animals reproduce by fission. During fission, the animal divides in two. Where there was one animal, there now are two. The two new animals grow quickly and soon are as large as the original animal.

Asexual reproduction can be very rapid. In paramecia, for example, fission may occur three times in one day. In other words, one animal will divide to form two, which will divide to form four, which will divide to form eight. Such rapid division happens only under the most ideal conditions, when there is lots of space and food, ideal temperatures, and no predators. If a paramecium reproduced only once a day—and all of its offspring lived to reproduce once a day—in less than four months the resulting population would take up as much space as the entire earth! It is indeed fortunate for the other creatures on earth that paramecia do not reproduce so fast.

Another type of asexual reproduction is budding. A new individual develops as an outgrowth, or bud, on an adult animal. One animal that commonly reproduces by budding is the hydra. This small relative of the jellyfish is a common inhabitant of lakes and ponds. It has a slender, tubelike body that is crowned by a mouth and a ring of delicate tentacles. Budding occurs at almost any time of year. The bud forms as a small projection of body tissues, about midway on the body wall of the adult hydra. Within two to three days, the bud has lengthened and developed into a young hydra, complete with a mouth surrounded by tiny tentacles. When the bud reaches a certain size, it breaks off from the parent and becomes independent.

Budding also is common among freshwater worms known as naidids. About midway along the worm's body a budding zone forms. Many new segments form in this zone. The front half and the back half of the worm develop into two complete worms—called daughter worms—and separate.

All offspring produced asexually look exactly like the parent animal. This is because they have inherited all their makeup (genetic material) from only one parent. In contrast, offspring resulting from sexual reproduction do not look exactly like either parent. They have some characteristics of each parent; they have inherited half their genetic material from the female and half from the male.

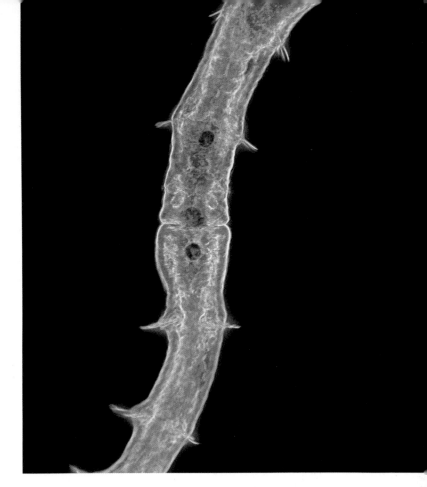

A stylaria, a freshwater worm, is about to divide into two separate worms.

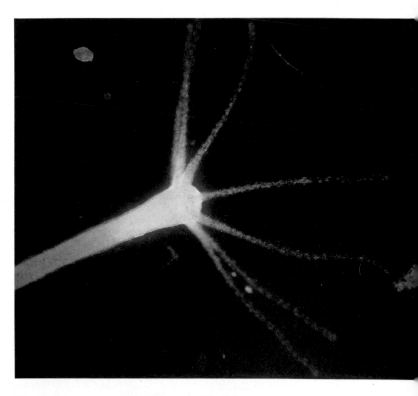

The hydra can reproduce either sexually by mating or asexually by budding.

63

Finding a Mate

Shortly before the first rays of sun begin to brighten the sky of New Guinea in the South Pacific, the greater bird-of-paradise can be heard. The males, crying "wawk-wawk-wawk," fly to a special tree in the forest. This is their display arena. What follows is one of the most magnificent sights of the animal world.

The males space themselves along the spreading branches. Some are high in the tree, others are lower. In the center of the group is the male with the longest plumes.

All of the males are brilliantly colored. A male greater bird-of-paradise is about the size of a crow. The upper side of his head and neck is a pale straw yellow. The throat area is dark metallic green. The body and wings are a rich brown. From beneath each wing springs a bunch of long, delicate feathers called plumes. At their base the plumes are red. Further along, the color changes—to orange, golden yellow, and, at the tips, a pale pinkish brown.

In the center of each bunch of plumes is one exceptionally long feather, called a wire, for it has a prominent wiry shaft. At one time these long feathers were in great demand as decorations for women's hats, and many birds were slaughtered to satisfy the needs of fashion.

The display behavior of the greater bird-of-paradise was first described by Alfred Russel Wal-

A pair of sticklebacks prepare to mate. The male's coloring has completely changed.

lace, the famous British naturalist, who visited New Guinea in the 1850s. Though many others have reported on and filmed the display since then, Wallace's description remains one of the most dramatic.

"A dozen or twenty full-plumaged male birds assemble together, raise up their wings, stretch out their necks, and elevate their exquisite plumes, keeping them in continual vibration. Between whiles they fly across from branch to branch in great excitement, so that the whole tree is filled with waving plumes in every variety of attitude and motion. . . . At the time of its excitement the wings are raised vertically over the back, the head is bent down and stretched out, and the long plumes are raised up and expanded till they form two magnificent golden fans, striped with deep red at the base, and fading off into the pale brown tint of the finely divided and softly waving points. The whole bird is then overshadowed by them, the crouching body, yellow head, and emerald-green throat forming but the foundation and setting to the golden glory which waves above. When seen in this attitude, the bird of paradise really deserves its name, and must be ranked as one of the most beautiful and most wonderful of living things."

As the males dance, the females move along the edges of the display arena. They are smaller than the males. Their feathers are a warm brown color, with no brilliant markings. They do not have plumes.

When a female enters the arena, the males end their rapid movements. They sit very still, with their heads bowed, mouths open, and eyes unblinking. Only the plumes may slowly rise and fall.

A greater bird–of–paradise spreads its tail feathers into two golden fans as the high point of its display behavior.

After a minute or so of maintaining this position, the males suddenly relax. They resume their normal stance. The plumes fall against the body. And the birds begin to preen (use their beak to arrange their feathers). The courtship dance is over.

Courtship is the finding and attracting of a member of the opposite sex. For many animals it is the first step in the process of sexual reproduction.

Courtship behavior differs from species to species. In many animals it is both complicated and fascinating. It may involve elaborate dances or other movements. It may involve special odors or songs. It may involve fighting or playing or kissing.

Some species undergo physical changes prior to courtship and breeding. The male stickleback, a small fish sometimes kept in home aquariums, changes color. Usually he is blueish or greenish, with a silver belly. But during breeding his back becomes blue and his belly turns bright red.

The male frigate bird normally has a pale pinkish throat sac. At mating time the sac turns bright red. The male forces air into the sac so that it is greatly enlarged.

Both males and females of the western grebe undergo changes in appearance. During the breeding season these water birds, which look a little like ducks, grow a showy crest of feathers on their heads. As they court, they shake their heads and make other movements that show off the special feathers. The western grebe also performs an interesting "dance on water." The male and female rise up and stand erect. In this stance they look a bit like penguins. Side by side, the two birds rush at high speed over the surface of the water. At the end of this sprint, they flop down with a loud splash and then dive deep into the lake. A weed dance may be part of the sequence. The grebes gather bits of weed from the water's bottom. When they surface, they present each other with the weed, which is the kind used to build their nests.

Western grebes dance across the water of a lake in their courtship ritual. They rush along, side by side, and come down with a loud splash.

The western sage grouse cock impresses the hen by inflating special air sacs to puff up, or "boom," his chest. He also fans out his tail.

The spring peeper is a tiny tree frog that has a high, whistling mating call. Its cheerful "peep" is one of the first signs that spring has arrived.

Like birds-of-paradise, western sage grouse choose a special arena in which to hold their courtship display. The males parade before the female grouse. After watching the strutting males, several of the females choose the most impressive male as the one with which they wish to mate.

The female grouse rush to claim the most attractive male—the male who dominates the group—because he is the finest bird, the one in best physical condition. By mating with him, the females are acting in the best interests of the species. Offspring from the mating will inherit the male's above-average qualities. This helps assure the survival of the best stock.

Among the animals that depend on vocal signals to attract mates are frogs. It is easy to know when frogs are mating, for their chorus of croaking fills the summer night with sound. Since more than a dozen species of frogs and toads may gather to breed in the same pond, it is important that each species has its own distinctive call.

Crickets and grasshoppers are among the insects that produce sound. But their courtship signals are not true songs, for they are not produced by the movement of air over vocal cords. Rather, crickets and grasshoppers produce sounds by rubbing together parts of the body. For instance, the male long-horned grasshopper produces sounds by rubbing the rough edge of his right forewing against his smooth left forewing.

Chemical signals are used by many species —from protozoans to mammals—to bring the sexes together or to stimulate the act of mating. These chemicals are called pheromones (FAIR-a-moans). Some species release their pheromones into the air. Others release them into the water or deposit them on the ground. Each species produces its own kind of pheromone.

For example, when the female of the lovely emperor butterfly is ready to mate, she settles on a leaf. She rhythmically protrudes and withdraws the end of her abdomen. On the abdomen are pheromone glands. They release the pheromone into the air. A male as distant as 200 or 300 feet can detect this scent. He follows the trail until he reaches the female. At this time, the male begins to release his own pheromone, which excites the female much as her odor excites him.

Most female mammals, like most other animals, have a definite breeding cycle. At a certain point in the cycle the eggs in the female's body are ready to be fertilized.The female is said to be in heat. At this time she accepts the advances of a male. Her body usually signals her readiness to mate by secreting pheromones. The females of some species are in heat for only a few weeks each year. In other species, they come into heat many times during a year.

Fireflies use another kind of chemical to attract mates. It is called luciferin (loo-SIF-er-in). When it combines with oxygen, light is produced. The male firefly begins the signaling. The female, who in most species is wingless and thus remains on the ground, replies with a slightly different flash of light. This identifies her and indicates her position. The male responds with another flash and the female again replies. This continues as the two insects slowly move closer.

Some animals even bring gifts to their mates. A male crow may present a stick to his mate. A male heron also brings twigs, which the female weaves into the nest. A penguin may give stones or snow. A tern may give a fish. Such behavior is not necessarily limited to the courtship period. While a female starling sits on her nest incubating the eggs, her mate may bring her flowers.

A snowy egret offers his mate a blade of reed grass as a token of his affection.

Mating habits, like courtship behavior, vary widely. In most species the two animals separate after mating and never see each other again. This is true with wolf spiders. In fact, the male leaves very quickly after he and the female mate—otherwise he may become a meal for the hungry female.

The male praying mantis doesn't run away. He remains, to be killed and eaten by the female mantis. His death is not in vain, however, for his body provides nourishment for the dozens of eggs laid by the female.

In some species, the male and female stay together for one or more seasons. Foxes, for example, stay together for most of the year. Their courtship, which takes place in January, begins after the male picks up and follows the female's scent, which was excreted on the ground as part of her urine. Their courtship is filled with chases, wrestling, and other playful behavior. The cubs are born about 50 days after mating. The female stays with them in the nest, or den, while the male brings her food. Later, when the cubs are old enough to move outdoors, the male protects them and helps teach them how to hunt. As autumn comes, the family breaks up. Each member of the family goes its separate way.

Some animals do mate for life. Albatrosses remain together until one of the partners dies. Many other seabirds also form permanent "marriages." Some captive geese never remate after the partner dies. Mammals that mate for life include beavers, badgers, mongooses, marmosets, and gibbons.

Fireflies light up this tree like an out-of-season Christmas display.

Parental Care

A mother cat rarely strays far from her young kittens. She keeps them in a warm, private spot, away from cold, dampness, and drafts. She feeds them at frequent intervals throughout the day. She washes them and gets rid of their wastes. When they grow older, she teaches them how to hunt and to defend themselves.

Not all parents are so caring of their offspring. In many species, parents never see nor have anything to do with their young. They release their eggs, then leave. In such cases, the number of eggs produced is astounding. A lobster may lay 15,000 eggs at a time. A starfish may release 2 million in a 2-hour period. A ling fish may lay 28 million. And a giant ocean sunfish may release 300 million. Of these eggs, only a small percentage eventually develop into mature animals. The others are eaten by predators or die because of unfavorable conditions.

Consider the plight of the oyster *Crassostrea virginica*, for example. This oyster, known as the Virginia or American oyster, is common along the eastern coast of North America and is a popular food for many people. A large female may release as many as 50 million eggs at a time. These are fertilized by sperm released into the sea water at the same time by a male oyster.

In a few days the fertilized eggs hatch. Many of the young, free-swimming oysters are eaten by predators. Others are swept out to sea and are unable to complete their life cycle. For, after a day or two, the oysters must settle down on some hard object—an empty shell, a stone, perhaps a discarded bottle or the remains of a sunken ship. They attach themselves to the object and remain there for the rest of their lives. If they settle in an area where the water contains little or no lime, they will not develop, for they need lime to build their shells. If there is too much pollution or not enough food, they will die. If too much fresh water flows into the area, thereby decreasing the saltiness of the water, they will die. The number of fertilized eggs that eventually become adult oysters is few indeed.

The simplest kind of parental care occurs when the female doesn't release her eggs just anywhere but, instead, chooses a place where they have a good chance of developing. Sea turtles, for example, do not release their eggs into the ocean waters. Instead, they swim to land, laboriously crawl up onto the beach, and bury their eggs in the sand. The eggs must be laid on land if they are to develop.

An ordinary house cat is one of the animal world's most protective and caring mothers.

The Pacific Ridley turtle comes ashore to lay eggs usually only one year out of every three years.

68

Conversely, spadefoot toads live on land but their eggs must be laid in water. Since these toads often live quite a distance from a pond or lake, they may lay their eggs in a puddle that formed after a heavy rain. This means that the young have only a short time in which to hatch and develop. They must turn into air-breathing land forms before the puddle dries up. Otherwise the young animals also dry up and die.

Many animals lay their eggs in a place where food will be available for the young. The granary weevil deposits her eggs in grains. When the young hatch, they feed on the grain. The elm-leaf beetle lays her eggs on the underside of elm leaves, which are then eaten by the young. Another beetle, the leaf-rolling weevil, makes more elaborate preparations for her offspring. She lays her eggs near the tip of a leaf, then rolls the leaf into a small cigar-shaped package. Next, she chews through the leaf near the stem, so that the package falls to the ground. When the young beetle hatches, it feeds on the rolled-up leaf that had been its nest. Each type of leaf-rolling weevil rolls its preferred leaf differently.

A greater degree of care is provided by parents who watch over their eggs until the young hatch. The cichlids (SIK-lids), a group of fish that includes such popular aquarium species as the tilapia, are an interesting example. Many species of cichlids are mouthbrooders. That is, they carry the fertilized eggs in their mouths until the young hatch. This may take a week or even longer. In some species, the parent does not eat during this period but lives on fat stored in its body. Other cichlids are able to feed without swallowing the eggs. Mouthbrooding is a fine adaptation for it helps protect the eggs from the many predators in the area.

Other cichlids, such as the African jewelfish, lay their eggs on rocks on the bottom. The parents take turns fanning the eggs with their fins. This provides the eggs with the oxygen they need for development and keeps them clean. When the young hatch, the parents take them into their mouths and carry them to a special pit they dug in the sand. The parents watch over their nursery. If a youngster strays out of the pit, a parent will carefully suck the young into its mouth and then blow it out into the nursery. Later, when the young are more developed, they will swim with their parents. Only when they are strong and able to take care of themselves will they move off and live on their own.

The greater care provided by animals such as cichlids means that an egg has a better chance of developing. As a result, fewer eggs are produced than

The oak leaf-rolling weevil lays her eggs (up to seven) only on the leaves of oaks and closely related trees and always rolls the leaves in a species-specific way.

is the case for animals that devote less care to their eggs. The female Atlantic salmon, who deposits her eggs on a gravelly stream floor, will lay about 10,000 eggs at a time. An African jewelfish will lay about 1,000 eggs. A mouthbrooding cichlid usually lays less than 100 eggs.

A different situation exists among social insects such as bees, ants, and wasps that live in large colonies. Here, great care generally is given to the eggs and, later, to the young insects. However, the care is not provided by the parents but by members of the colony called workers. A colony of *Vespa* wasps (often called "hornets" or "yellow jackets"), for example, will have one queen. She lays all the eggs. The eggs are placed in closely packed cells within the colony's papery nest. When the young wasps hatch, they are fed by the workers. Food consists mainly of finely chewed pieces of insect prey. The nest is so constructed that the young wasps' other needs—oxygen, protection, and so on—are also provided.

All the animals discussed so far have behavior patterns that are inherited. They are not learned. Such inherited, unlearned behavior patterns are called instinct. The young animals know, without being shown, what foods to eat, how to eat, and how to recognize and escape from predators.

Other young animals, especially young birds and mammals, have to learn a great deal of their behavior. They have to learn how to find food, how to defend themselves, how to communicate. These animals depend on their parents to teach them. Usually, the amount of time parents spend teaching their young is related to how complicated the behavior of that animal is. The more complicated the patterns of behavior, the longer the period of parental care and supervision. Baby swans will stay with their parents for a year. Young camels stay with their mother for four years. Chimpanzees will stay with their mother for up to 10 years.

During a chimp's first three years, it is almost as dependent as a human child. It depends on its mother for food and protection. It sleeps with her and rides on her back as she travels from place to place. By the end of the third year, the young chimp gathers its own food and makes its own nest. But it continues to spend much of its time with its mother. It continues to learn from her and from other adults in the band.

Paper wasps build a new cell for each new egg. Later, the cells are enlarged.

A baby chimpanzee is as dependent upon its mother for care as is a human child. It will not become completely independent until it has reached its teens.

Salmon will challenge any obstacle in their way to reach the freshwater streams in which they spawn. Many salmon die on the dangerous and exhausting journey from the sea. Yet enough survive to continue the species.

The young chimp may, for example, learn how to "fish" for termites. It watches while adults in the band break branches off a tree, remove the leaves, then stick the "fishing rods" into termite holes. It is doubtful that a young chimp would become skilled at—or even attempt—this complicated task if it had not watched older chimps doing it.

While mammals generally give birth to their young in some sort of nest or den, birds are the champion nest builders. Most birds build nests in which they lay their eggs, incubate the eggs, and care for the newly hatched fledglings. Each species of bird builds its own kind of nest. Nest building is inherited, but it may be improved upon through experience. Among birds that build intricate nests, the young usually do not build nests that are as fine as those of older birds. But after several years of nest building, a bird becomes an expert at the craft.

In the nest the baby birds are protected from cold and from enemies. They are fed frequently by their parents. But not all birds build nests. Nevertheless non-nest builders may show as much care as or even greater care than some nest builders. For instance, the king penguins, which live on the ice of the South Polar region, do not build nests. Instead, the male penguin has a pocketlike fold of skin on his

A male king penguin uses his beak to push the egg laid by his mate onto his webbed feet. He then covers the egg with a fold of skin and incubates it for 64 days in the harsh Antarctic spring.

belly. He holds the egg on his large webbed feet and covers it with the fold of skin. For 64 days, he incubates the egg. During this time he cannot eat. He lives on fat stored in his body. As a result, he loses as much as a third of his weight. Soon after the egg hatches, the female penguin returns and takes charge of the baby. Her mate is free to swim off in search of a well-earned meal.

One of the most important things that a young bird learns from its parents are its songs. Each species has its own distinctive songs. There are even songs special to a particular region. Some basic guidelines for singing are inherited. A bird raised alone will sing, though only a very simple song. If during a crucial period of development it hears records of its species' songs, it will imitate the sounds. If, instead, it hears the song of another species—even a closely related

species—it will not learn the song.

Not all learning by birds and mammals is done with the help of parents. Much is trial-and-error learning. That is, the animal tries something. It may or may not work, but the animal will remember what happened. For example, a young pigeon instinctively knows how to drink. But it doesn't know what to drink. This it learns by trial and error. The ability of the pigeon to fly, or the horse to run, or the squirrel to scamper up a tree also involves trial and error. The basic movements are inherited but practice is needed to move skillfully under all sorts of conditions.

Among young mammals, games frequently are part of the learning process. Young deer will chase one another around trees, perfecting their ability to run and leap. Fox cubs will stalk one another, pouncing and fighting as practice for hunting. Such activities may seem violent, but the cubs do not hurt one another. They know how hard they can bite or hit each other without doing damage. Besides, their mother is usually nearby, ready to interfere if things get too rough.

Food for Baby Mammals

Baby mammals get the best care in the world. As we have seen, other kinds of baby animals may get no care at all. For example, a newborn butterfly or turtle never even sees its parents. But baby mammals are cared for by their mothers—sometimes with help from their fathers—until they are almost fully grown. This care is absolutely necessary. A newborn mammal cannot get along by itself. It needs its mother to care for it, feed it, and train it.

All baby mammals are fed milk, which is produced by the mother's mammary glands. It is these glands that give mammals their name. No other animal has mammary glands.

The female mammal doesn't produce milk all the time. Her body makes milk right after she gives birth. The milk provides all the food needed by her babies. It contains proteins, fats, sugars, minerals, and vitamins. However, the composition of the milk varies from mammal to mammal. For example, whale milk contains 5 times as much fat as cow's milk and 16 times more than horse's milk. However, cow's milk and horse's milk contain more than 10 times as much sugar as whale's milk.

In general, young animals that receive the milk with the highest protein content grow the fastest. A porpoise mother's milk contains 10 times as much protein as a human mother's milk. A baby porpoise doubles its birth weight in about 1½ weeks. A human baby takes about 26 weeks to double its birth weight.

Some mammal mothers, such as cows and horses, stand up while their babies feed (nurse). Others, such as lions and seals, lie on their sides. Still others, such as raccoons, nurse in a seated position. The position depends on the location of the openings of the mammary glands—the nipples or teats. Different mammals have different numbers of nipples. In general, the greater the number of young born at one time, the greater the number of nipples on the mother's body.

Dolphin and whale mothers give birth to and raise their young in water. These mammals have a special ring of muscle around the teat. When the baby takes the teat into its mouth, it does not have to suck for milk. Instead, the ring of muscles contracts,

Colts are on their thin legs minutes after birth. They follow their mothers around, nursing often.

A dromedary (one-humped camel) nurses her offspring for at least a year. The young dromedary remains close to its mother for the first four years of its life.

73

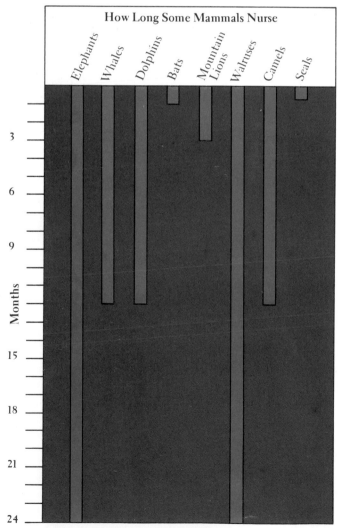

How Long Some Mammals Nurse

Elephants, Whales, Dolphins, Bats, Mountain Lions, Walruses, Camels, Seals

Months

3
6
9
15
18
21
24

A newborn elephant stands more than three feet tall and weighs between 200 and 300 pounds.

squirting the milk down the baby's throat. This adaptation is useful because dolphin and whale babies cannot take slow meals. They must feed quickly, for soon they must rise to the water's surface to breathe.

Different mammals nurse their young for different lengths of time. A cat nurses its kittens for about 8 weeks. An elephant nurses its young for as long as 2 years. This does not mean that a baby cat or a baby elephant eats nothing else during this time. As it—or any other young mammal—grows its first teeth, it can begin to change over to the diet that is typical of the species. This transition from milk to solid foods is called weaning.

The mother plays an important role in introducing her offspring to solid foods. In meat-eating species, such as lions and other members of the cat family, the mother must catch and kill an animal for food. Her young do not yet know how to hunt. Nor are they quick enough or strong enough to chase and catch another animal. If the prey caught by the mother is small enough, she carries it back to the nest. Foxes and domestic cats do this. Other animals, such as wolves, catch prey that is too large to be carried back to the nest. The mother bites off and swallows chunks of meat. When she is back with her young, she regurgitates the food. That is, the food passes from her stomach back out through her mouth. It may have been partly digested by the mother's body,

A doe will risk her own life to protect her helpless fawns. She will lead a predator on a chase away from her offspring.

Piglets follow their mother around and attempt to nurse but only succeed when she lies down.

making it easier for the young to eat. Another technique is used by the grasshopper mouse. This mouse eats insects. Normally it eats the front part of the insect first and, later, the back part. The parents of weaning young, however, often will eat only the front part of the prey. They leave the back part in or near the nest for their children to find and eat.

In plant-eating mammals, such as cows and horses, getting solid food is easier. The young simply travel with the mother and feed where she does. In most plant-eating mammals, little help is given by the mother. An exception is found among apes and monkeys. A mother chimpanzee, for example, may hand food to her child. Or she may let the child take partly chewed food from her mouth.

Some mammals, such as horses, deer, and antelopes, are well developed at birth. They can eat plant matter almost immediately. They receive part of their nourishment from the plants and part from their mothers' milk. Other mammals, such as house mice, kangaroos, and most meat-eaters, are poorly developed at birth. They require a long period of nursing before they can begin to be weaned.

This chapter looked at the ways different animals have assured the continuance of life for their species. It followed the process from finding a mate to caring for the young. The next chapter looks at how different species live together in a shared environment.

Living Together

In the warm waters of the Caribbean there is a world unsurpassed in beauty. It is a world of brilliant colors—reds, greens, oranges, purples, and blues—as well as delicate pastel shades. It is a world of strange shapes and dramatic patterns. It is a world filled with animals as fascinating as their names: blue tangs, parrot fish, lettuce corals, sea fans, striped grunts.

This world is a coral reef. The animal responsible for its existence is a coral polyp, which looks like a miniature sea anemone. The largest polyps are no bigger than peas. It take millions of them, working generation after generation for hundreds of years, to build a reef. Each polyp forms a limestone shell around its tiny body. When it dies, another polyp settles on the outside of the shell and builds its own shell. This process is repeated over and over again. The only living part of the coral reef is the surface. The lower, inner part consists of the deposits left by polyps of an earlier time.

Many different shapes of coral live in the same area. Some look like lettuce leaves. Others are round with grooved surfaces and resemble brains. Others look like branching antlers of an elk or like clusters of fat fingers. In part, the shape of the coral is determined by the species of polyp that builds the coral. And in part it is determined by conditions in the environment. Fragile forms, such as sea fans, develop on the ocean floor. Hardier forms, such as elkhorn and finger corals, develop near the surface.

Living in the nooks and crannies formed by the coral are worms, sponges, sea urchins, eels, and other creatures. Spiny lobsters and crabs crawl along the bottom. Schools of fish swim through the forestlike surroundings.

The plants and animals that live in this environment effect, and are affected by, each other. They form a community—a group of organisms that live in a particular area.

There are many different types of communities on earth. Often they are named after the animal or plant that is dominant or most noticeable. Thus we have the coral reef community, the mangrove swamp community, the sagebrush community, the pine forest community. A community may exist within another community. For example, the organisms that live in the soil of the pine forest community

Grunts and squirrelfish live together in harmony among the coral of a Caribbean reef.

A fallen log may provide a sheltered home for many insects; toads, snakes, and lizards; a small mammal; and even a bird family.

This mangrove swamp in the Florida Everglades is home to many kinds of fish and birds.

make up a soil community. A rotting log on the forest floor may form another community. A cave within the forest may also have its own community of organisms.

Every community depends on the flow of energy from one organism to another. The source of energy in every community is the sun. Green plants store this energy in food that they produce from water and carbon dioxide. Without green plants, there would be no food. All the animals that live on earth, including people, would be unable to live. An animal must consume its food either by eating green plants or by eating an animal that ate a green plant. It then breaks down the food, releasing the energy needed to keep its body working.

The flow of energy from one organism to another is called a food chain. This is a series of relationships based on who eats what. At the beginning of any food chain are green plants. In the coral reef community and other ocean communities, these usually are microscopic algae (AL-gee) that float in the surface waters. There are billions upon billions of them. The algae are eaten by swarms of protozoans and other small animals that also float in the surface waters. These animals form the second link in a coral reef food chain. The next link may be a small fish that feeds on the floating organisms. It, in turn, may be caught and eaten by a sea anemone or by another, larger fish.

Food chains in other communities are similar. In a grasslands community, various grasses are the food producers. Rabbits eat the grass. Red-tailed hawks eat the rabbits. Crows feed on the dead bodies of the hawks.

Few animals rely on only one species for their food. A red-tailed hawk eats not only rabbits but also mice, rats, squirrels, moles, shrews, snakes, and insects. Usually, several species compete for the same food. Foxes, coyotes, and owls compete with hawks for rabbits, mice, and other prey. Thus, a community really has a number of interrelated food chains. These make up a food web, which often is very complex.

Members of the species that live in the same community form a population. The red-tailed hawks in the grasslands form a population. So does each species of rabbit, mouse, fox, and crow. In a stable community, the number of animals in each population remains about the same, though there may be seasonal and annual variations. If, for instance, there is a plentiful food supply, rabbits may reproduce more rapidly, thereby increasing their population. Hawks will find lots of rabbits to eat and they, too, will reproduce faster. But if the hawks become too plentiful, they will eat the rabbits faster than the rabbits can reproduce themselves. The rabbit population will drop, and there will not be enough food for all the hawks. Then some hawks will starve to death. Others will live but be too weak to reproduce. In time, these conditions will result in a decrease in the hawk population. The rabbits will then increase again. Thus a cycle is set up in which populations within a community rise and fall but remain in overall balance.

The members of a population may be found scattered randomly throughout the community, they may be distributed more or less evenly throughout the community, or they may live together in groups. Foxes, hawks, and coyotes form family groups consisting of an adult male, an adult female, and their young. European rabbits form larger groups; many of them will live together in a communal burrow. Crows form large flocks. Owls are solitary creatures; they join together only to mate.

A major advantage of living in a group is increased protection. When one member of the group spots danger, it can alert all the other members. Many predators will not attack a group. A hawk, for example, will attack a solitary starling. However, it won't attack a flock of starlings; it might injure its wings as it plunges down among them.

Among animals that live in groups there is a definite social organization. Each member of the group has a certain position and a certain role. For example, in a European rabbit family, the male defends the territory and his family against outsiders; the female feeds and cares for the young. In a termite colony, which may contain a million or more members, two termites—the queen and king—are responsible for reproduction. The soldiers, which have large, strong jaws, protect the colony from enemies. The workers build the nest, gather food, and care for the young.

Sagebrush flourishes in the western United States on semi-arid plains and nearby mountain slopes. **Gambel oak** is seen in the background.

Among chickens, often only those highest in the pecking order mate, thus passing on their hardy, aggressive characteristics.

In some animal societies, the group is dominated by one individual. Among chickens, for example, pecking orders are common. The bird at the top of the pecking order is the most aggressive. It pecks all the other birds in the group but rarely gets pecked itself. The bird at the bottom of the pecking order is the least aggressive. It gets pecked the most. The chicken at the top of the order gets to eat first, has first choice of a roosting spot, and so on. But the pecking order is not permanent. If one chicken becomes weak or ages, it is forced into a lower spot in the order. There is one pecking order among the male chickens, another among the females.

A social group may be composed of more than one type of animal. This is quite common among fishes of the coral reef. A school of grunts may include some snappers and a few yellowtails. This type of group is particularly interesting because animals of different species, in order to move together, must recognize the same signals.

In many communities, even closer relationships may exist between members of two species. Partnerships may form in which both animals benefit. The three-toed sloth of South America has such a relationship with a small insect called the sloth moth. Tiny green algae live in the sloth's fur. This is very helpful to the sloth, for it helps camouflage the otherwise defenseless sloth. However, too much algae can harm the sloth. The sloth moth, which lives only in the fur of the three-toed sloth, feeds on the algae, keeping its population down to a safe level.

Sometimes, members of two different species have a close relationship in which one benefits but the other is harmed. This is called parasitism. Segmented worms called leeches are parasites. They have large suckers on their front and back ends. A leech will move through a pond until it comes in contact with its victim, called a host—a frog, for example. With its suckers the leech attaches itself to the skin of the frog. Using its mouth parts, it pierces the frog's skin and begins to feed on its blood. In many cases, the leech remains attached to the frog until the frog dies. However, frogs have developed a way to get rid of the leeches. They sit in the sun. The leeches cannot stand the heat and either detach themselves from the frogs or die. The frogs aren't fond of the heat, either, but it's better than being sucked dry by leeches.

This chapter looks at five different examples of animals living together.

First observed are howler monkeys, who live together in bands of some 20 to 35 members—each with a specific role to play.

Next, the hermit crab is seen finding its borrowed home, then sharing it with other animals that can be of benefit to it. The hermit crab's relationship with these other animals is often also

Sloths, which live in Central and South America, eat, sleep, mate, and even give birth clinging upside down to trees with their hooklike claws.

This freshwater leech has attached its head sucker to the tail of a fish. It will pierce the fish's skin and feed on its blood.

beneficial to the other animals, but this is not the case in the parasitic relationships formed by certain protozoans discussed in the third section.

"Life in the Mountains of Montana" follows the many animals of this wilderness community through a whole year, showing how each species reacts to seasonal changes. Then, in the last section, a very different community is explored—Cathedral Cave in Kentucky.

While each of these examples is different, in each case the animals must live together in order to survive.

A Band of Monkeys

Twenty-one howler monkeys lie sleeping high in a tree in a tropical forest in Central America. They are all members of one group, or band. There are 3 adult males, 5 adult females without babies, 3 mothers with babies, and 7 juveniles (youngsters who no longer are babies but are still not fully grown).

When morning comes, the howlers awake. Soon they begin chattering among themselves. "Where should we go today?" they seem to say. "Where is a good spot to eat?"

One of the males clucks, "Come this way." He moves along the tree limbs, steps onto another tree, and soon is running quickly through the trees of the forest. The other members of the band follow, one behind the other. The mothers, their babies clutching tightly to their fur, bring up the rear.

When the howlers reach a tree filled with tasty fruit or tender leaves and twigs, they settle down to eat. Breakfast is a leisurely meal, taking as long as two hours. The mothers feed their babies. The juveniles practice their swinging technique. Clucks, grunts, and other vocal signals are frequently heard.

In the middle of the day, when the temperatures are high, the howlers rest for a few hours. At least the adults do. The younger animals play, wrestling and noisily chasing one another through the trees. By midafternoon the band is on the move again. They head for another tree in their territory, where they eat their second meal of the day. As darkness falls, they move to a lodge tree—a favorite tree for sleeping in—and settle down for the night. Some rest on thick branches. Others curl up in crotches formed by a branch and the tree trunk. Each monkey uses its tail as an anchor to keep it from falling off the tree during the night.

Other animals in the area may not have heard the howlers arrive. Also, the dense foliage hides animals from one another. But all the other animals learn of the howlers' presence early the following morning. One of the first things a member of the howler band does on awakening is give forth a spectacular roar. Don Felix de Azara, who observed the howlers of Paraguay in the late 1700s, wrote of "their powerful, melancholy, harsh, insufferable, and indescribable voice." Frank M. Chapman, who studied howlers in this century, had this to say about the howling: "Beginning as a low grunt, it grows louder, rapid, more incisive, and quickly rises to an overpowering, ferocious-sounding roar."

The low-pitched howl carries far. One scientist estimated that a howler's call can carry 1½ miles through the jungle. The roars of three howlers kept in a London pet shop could be heard 3 miles away.

Usually, one male member of the band does the calling. Sometimes, several males howl at the same time. Occasionally, the entire band cries. The voice box, or larynx (LAR-inks), of a female howler monkey is not as well developed as that of a male. As a result, her calls are not as loud as those of a male and, in fact, sound rather like the bark of a fox terrier.

The purpose of the call is to communicate with other animals in the area. It warns them that the band is present. It says, "This is our territory."

Toward threats from below, the howlers also have two other types of defensive behavior. They may break off dead branches from a tree and drop them on the intruder. Or they may excrete wastes on the intruder. C. Ray Carpenter, who conducted a famous field study of the behavior of howler monkeys on Barro Colorado Island in the Panama Canal Zone, described this second behavior:

The roar of a male howler monkey, laying claim to his band's territory, is one of the loudest sounds in the tropical forest where howlers live.

Leaves and twigs form part of the howler's diet.

A howler monkey may hang by its tail to reach food.

"I would usually be sitting quietly observing the animals as they were in the trees above me. Either seen or unseen, an individual would slowly approach to the place directly above me or as near-by as possible, and then would release excrement, either urine or fecal matter or both. When the act was completed, the individual would usually quickly withdraw. While observing animals from within a blind located under the line of march of a group, I have seen as many as half of the animals release fecal matter on the blind as they crossed over it."

Whenever possible, the band tries to avoid danger. Often, the tree on which a band of howlers is feeding is invaded by a group of red spider monkeys or capuchin monkeys. Although the howlers are bigger and more powerful than the other two species, they are less aggressive. Either the two groups ignore each other or the howlers depart, moving on to another tree and leaving the first to the invaders.

Carpenter observed one band for 22 days, to see how widely it ranged and what type of trees and foods it preferred. The band, which consisted of 26 howlers, had a territory of about 300 acres. On the average, the band covered a distance of about 600 feet a day. One day, it traveled only 150 feet. On another day it traveled 2,400 feet. The centers of its activity were favorite food trees, lodge trees, and resting spots. There also were preferred routes, which the howlers obviously remembered from previous wanderings.

A band's territory has definite boundaries. Each band is familiar with other howler bands that occupy neighboring territories, but each band avoids the others. If two bands do meet—perhaps because one has strayed into the territory of the other—a mutually threatening display of noise takes place.

Howlers belong to a group of New World monkeys known as the "hand-tailed monkeys." The name is appropriate, for a howler uses its tail as a fifth hand. It is used primarily as a grasping organ, to keep the animal from falling. As such it is used for many activities: it may be coiled around a branch so that the monkey can dangle 10 or even 15 minutes while picking and eating fruit from a lower branch. It can assist the hands as the howler climbs up a vine. The tail also is used to drive off pesky insects and for grooming.

Howlers spend almost all their time in trees. They descend to the forest floor only if absolutely necessary. If a baby falls to the ground, its mother rushes down to rescue it. The other members of the band howl loudly, presumably to frighten away predators that may be lurking on the ground. Sometimes, a band descends to the ground if it faces attack by other animals or if it is being forced out of its territory by another band of howlers. More and more, bands are being forced to the ground because people are clearing the forests in which the howlers live.

Carpenter was told by some Panamanians that they had seen howlers swim across a river. The howlers, they said, swam like people do, making a series of overhand strokes with their arms. Carpenter released a howler on a small island to see what it would do. Three hours later, the monkey was gone. It had swum back to Barro Colorado Island, a distance of 50 feet.

A howler band averages between 20 and 35 members. Usually there are more females than males. The group has a definite organization. Members have specific roles to play based on their age, sex, and, possibly, their personality. The males lead the group, defend the territory, and defend members against outsiders. The females' primary role is the care of the young, although the males may also participate in this activity to some extent. The youngsters have no specific roles. But as they grow they learn the patterns of behavior that are appropriate in their group. Adults are very lenient with the young howlers, but discipline increases as the juveniles near maturity. Play-fighting, for example, is allowed unless it is dangerous. Then a growl from an adult male quickly brings such behavior to an end.

As in a human community, subgroups form within the howler band. Some of these last for months or even years. Others are temporary. The longest-lasting and closest subgroup is that of a mother and her child. At first, the infant is almost completely dependent on its mother for food,

Howler monkeys will jump from tree to tree when they can find no easier route.

protection, and movement from place to place. For the first month of its life the baby is carried on its mother's belly. Then it begins to ride around the base of the mother's tail. If it falls, it immediately starts crying. But when it is picked up and held closely by its mother, it makes a purring sound much like that of a contented kitten. At night the mother holds her infant close, keeping it warm and protecting it from rain.

At about 6 months a young howler begins to move about on its own. But its mother still helps it over difficult crossings. When they come to a spot where a jump of several feet must be made, the mother wraps her tail around the end of the branch on the first tree, then jumps and with her hands grabs hold of the branch on the second tree. She then remains suspended between the two branches so her child can climb over her back. When the child has crossed, the mother pulls herself up onto the second tree and hurries after the other members of the band.

Temporary subgroups include a group of juvenile playmates and a group of defending males. Another subgroup forms when a female gives birth. The other females gather round to chatter and view the newborn baby. Some may touch the infant with their mouths or hands.

84

The females often stay together. They feed in the same part of a tree and sleep close together at night. But close relationships between females and males are rare, except when mating. A female will mate with any male in the band. The males also show no preference in mating. This communal kind of sexual relationship is believed to play an important role in maintaining the harmony that exists between members of the band.

There is very little fighting among members of the band. The males rarely fight among themselves. They do not fight over a female. Nor do they try to dominate one another. As the group moves through the forest, the males explore possible ways of getting from one tree to the next. Howlers do not like to jump from tree to tree and will avoid this if they can. The males look for a way to move from the end branches of one tree directly onto the end branches of an adjacent tree. When one of the males finds an easy path, he makes a deep clucking sound. The females and youngsters begin to follow him. The other males stop their explorations and also follow. The leader-follower relationship changes from tree to tree. No one male is always in the lead.

Howlers have two major methods of communication: vocal signals and postures. Vocal signals include the distress cry and purring of a baby, the

A young howler monkey lets out a roar. Perhaps he has found a good path through the trees.

bark of an upset female, the howls, clucking and disciplinary growl of a male. Young howlers make chirping sounds when they want to play. A mother will wail when her baby falls. And a male will grunt when faced with an unusual situation.

Posturing—assuming a certain pose—may be used when a howler senses a disturbance. He will crouch. Other howlers, noticing him do this, will stop moving and crouch, too. All will remain still until the first animal moves. Since he is the one that sees the disturbance, he is the one that controls the group's actions.

Gestures and facial expressions also are used for communication. When a howler waves its arms, reaches to caress another, winks its eyes, or wiggles its tongue, it is saying something that is understood by another howler.

Each day brings new experiences and challenges to the howler monkeys in their tree-top world. By facing the day together, as a group, they improve their chances of survival. Their cooperation with one another, their concern for each other's welfare, and their peacefulness are traits that human beings can admire.

The black howler monkey (*Alouatta caraya*) (shown here) and the red howler monkey (*A. seniculus*) (shown in the previous pictures) may live in the same area, but they do not interbreed.

85

The Hermit Crab and Its Partners

Hermit crabs don't do a very good job of living up to their name. True, like human hermits, a hermit crab avoids others of its own kind. But it willingly shares its home with worms, sponges, sea anemones, and other animals.

A hermit crab's back does not have a hard shell covering. To protect this part of its body, the crab moves into an empty snail shell. It attaches itself to this home by means of hooklike appendages.

As the crab moves around, it carries its home with it. The abdomen usually remains in the shell but the front part of the crab's body is out in the open. However, at the first sign of danger, the crab withdraws its entire body into the shell. Only the one large claw remains visible, as it blocks the shell's opening.

Some hermit crabs share their shell with a ragworm, *Nereis fucata*. At first glance the worm seems to be the only one who benefits from the relationship. It lies in the shell waiting for the hermit crab to find a morsel of food. Then the ragworm sticks its head out of the shell, grabs some of the food, and retreats with it into the shell.

Why does the hermit crab allow this? Isn't the worm intruding in the crab's home? No. The situation is quite the reverse. It is the crab who has intruded. The worm was there first.

A snail shell becomes empty when the snail dies. In the ocean world, many snails are killed by fish. For example, a dogfish that spies a snail crawling along will quickly bite off its head and any other part that is not enclosed in the shell. The part of the snail within the shell is left behind. If a ragworm finds these remains, it settles in the shell. As it eats the remains of the snail, an empty space forms within the shell. The hermit crab spots this space and tries it on for size. If the house fits, the crab stays. The least it can do is give some food to the first tenant.

Some hermit crabs share their homes with sponges. The crab lives within the shell, the sponge lives on the outside. If possible, the crab will choose a shell that already has a sponge growing on it. If the crab cannot find such a shell, it moves into one without a sponge. Then it looks for a partner. When the hermit crab finds the right kind of sponge, it removes it from a rock or other object on which it is living and places it on its shell.

As the sponge grows, it covers more and more of the shell. This hides the shell—and the hermit crab—from animals that might eat the crab, or even

A hermit crab may trail a **sea anemone** behind it (top), or it may be nearly engulfed in the protective covering of a **sponge** (bottom).

the shell. (Very few animals eat sponges.) In turn, as the hermit crab moves along, it sets up water currents that carry food particles to the sponge.

Many hermit crabs choose sea anemones instead of sponges as their external (outside) partners. Most predators avoid sea anemones. The anemones have poisonous stinging cells on their tentacles that inflict nasty wounds and can easily kill small fish. Thus an animal that might otherwise eat hermit crabs will avoid ones that live in shells covered with anemones. The anemones—there may be several on top of one shell—also camouflage the shell, making it difficult for a potential predator to spot.

As the crab feeds or moves along, the sea anemone bends backward. Its tentacles brush along the ocean floor, picking up bits of food dislodged by the movements of the crab.

Hermit crabs and sea anemones will take extraordinary measures to achieve and maintain their relationship. A crab that outgrows its shell must search for a bigger shell. When it finds one and moves in, it may encourage the sea anemone from its old home to move onto the new home. It strokes and prods the sea anemone until the anemone relaxes and detaches itself from the old home. The crab then picks up the anemone and places it on the new shell. The anemone must recognize the crab, since it does not hurt the crab with its stinging cells. Hermit crabs that live with sponges also have been observed transferring their partners. Ragworms, however, are left behind. Chances are, the new home already has a ragworm living in it.

In some relationships, it is the sea anemone, not the hermit crab, that seeks out a partner. For example, the sea anemone *Calliactis parasitica* can recognize a hermit crab shell. If the anemone is resting on a rock or other seafloor object, it will first attach its tentacles to the shell. Then the animal detaches its base from the rock and moves onto the shell. When the base is attached to the shell, the tentacles are released.

This hermit crab has selected a moon snail shell for its home. Perhaps it will move into a larger shell before seeking out a sea anemone or a sponge to share its living quarters.

One hermit crab, *Pagurus prideauxi*, doesn't have to hunt for a new home to protect its growing body. Its partner is the cloak anemone. Unlike other anemones, which settle on the top side of the shell, the cloak anemone attaches itself to the underside, just behind the opening. As it grows, it gradually encircles the shell, until it completely surrounds the shell's opening. The hermit crab moves its head and claws in and out through the circle formed by the bottom of the cloak anemone's body. As the anemone gets bigger, it actually forms a tube that extends forward from the shell. This increases the size of the hermit crab's home, thus freeing the crab from the need to change shells as it grows. As the crab grows, part of its abdomen remains in the shell and part lies within the tube formed by the anemone.

Some deep-sea hermit crabs form partnerships with anemones that have light-producing organs. Exactly what, if any, benefit the crab receives from this is not yet known. Does the light help the crab see prey? Does it help the crab attract members of the opposite sex? This is one of the mysteries of life still to be solved by scientists.

A Protozoan with Two Homes

"It was most disgusting to feel soft wingless insects about an inch long, crawling over one's body. Before sucking they are quite thin, but afterward they become round and bloated with blood, and in this state are easily crushed. One which I caught was very empty. When placed on a table, and though surrounded by people, if a finger was presented, the bold insect would immediately protrude its sucker, make a charge, and if allowed, draw blood. No pain was caused by the wound. It was curious to watch its body during the act of sucking, as in less than ten minutes it changed from being flat as a wafer to a globular form."

The writer was Charles Darwin, the great nineteenth-century naturalist. He was traveling through South America in the 1830s when the insect attacked him.

The insect was a species of cone-nosed bug. Although it may have been interesting to watch, it could have been deadly. It might have been carrying a protozoan with the name *Trypanosoma cruzi*. This one-celled animal—commonly called a trypanosome (TRIP-a-na-sohm)—causes Chagas' disease. The disease is named after Carlos Chagas, who discovered the protozoan in 1909 in Brazil. (In Charles Darwin's day, people had not yet realized that insects could transmit disease.)

Trypanosomes are flagellates (FLAJ-a-lates)—protozoans with long, slender, whiplike structures called flagella (singular: flagellum). The flagella are used for moving about.

During part of its life cycle this trypanosome (abbreviated as *T. cruzi*) lives as a parasite in the intestine of a bug. At least 25 species of bugs carry this parasite. These bugs are found mainly in South and Central America. One species, the Mexican bedbug, is common in Mexico and the American southwest.

The Mexican bedbug (above) carries *Trypanosoma cruzi* (below), which causes Chagas' disease, in its intestine as a parasite.

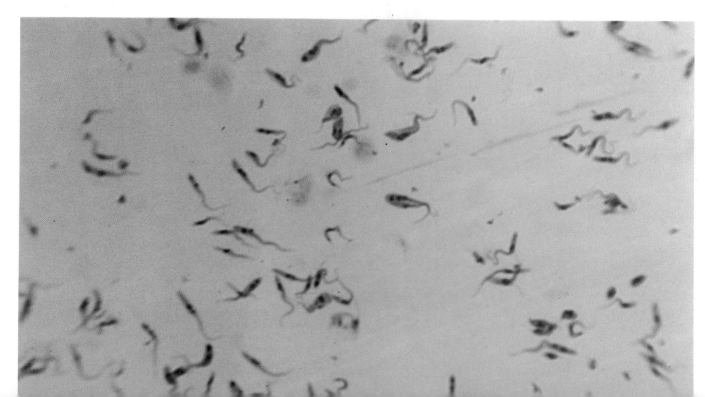

The bugs that carry *T. cruzi* feed on the blood of warm-blooded animals, including people. They often invade homes in search of blood. When they find a victim, they bite into its skin and begin to suck up blood. As they feed, they may also excrete wastes. The wastes, containing some *T. cruzi,* remain on the person's (or animal's) skin, next to the bite mark. If the person then scratches the bite and opens the wound, some of the waste comes in contact with the person's bloodstream. The parasites in the wastes may then move into the blood. Or, as the person scratches the bite, some of the parasites may stick to his hand. Then if the person rubs his eyes or puts his hand to his mouth, the parasites enter the body through the eyes or mouth. Once in the person's body, the parasites reproduce, thereby starting a new colony.

If *T. cruzi* enters the body through the eyes, the eyes become swollen and inflamed. If it enters through the bite on the skin, a small reddish-purple sore may form. Fever may develop.

Over several weeks, the symptoms (signs of the disease) may disappear. However, the disease often becomes chronic—that is, symptoms continually recur and the person never recovers his former strength. He will suffer from fevers, skin rashes, swellings of the glands and other body parts, and anemia. A heart condition may develop, resulting in chest pains and shortness of breath. Sometimes changes occur in the nervous system and the person has convulsions or suffers from sleepiness. Often, the symptoms eventually go away by themselves. But sometimes the disease grows increasingly worse, until the person dies.

Between five and ten percent of the people who get Chagas' disease eventually die from it. So far, no effective treatment for the disease has been found. It is possible, however, partially to control the insect population through the use of insecticides.

Two close relatives of *T. cruzi* also are dangerous human parasites. These species, *T. gambiense* and *T. rhodesiense,* are found in Africa. The disease they cause is known as African sleeping sickness.

Like *T. cruzi,* the African trypanosomes have two hosts. The insect host is a fly—the tsetse (TSET-see) fly. This is a small fly only about ¼ to ½ inch long. It has a thin, hard snout, or proboscis. This needlelike structure is used for piercing skin and sucking blood.

The trypanosomes live in the tsetse fly's saliva. When the fly bites a person, its saliva mixes with the person's blood. In this way, the parasites are introduced into the person's bloodstream. The victim

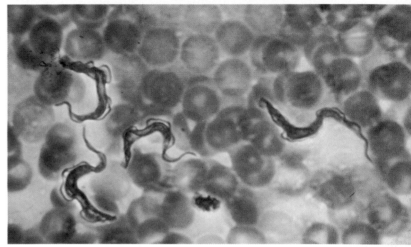

The tsetse fly (top) carries in its saliva **trypanosomes** (bottom) that cause African sleeping sickness. When the fly bites a victim, the trypanosomes may enter the victim's bloodstream.

is not immediately aware that he has been infected, but as the parasites reproduce and increase in numbers, the body begins to react to their presence. In about 10 to 15 days, the person begins to experience fever, headaches, and swelling of glands. Sleepiness is the next symptom, followed by paralysis of some parts of the body, convulsions, and, finally, coma.

If medical help is sought while the sleeping sickness is still in its early stages, drugs usually are effective in curing the disease. However, once the person reaches the stage where he is experiencing extreme sleepiness, chances of recovery are poor.

Other species of trypanosomes infect other mammals. In Africa they are responsible for fatal diseases of both game animals and domestic animals, including antelopes, camels, cattle, horses, and sheep.

The tiny protozoans that cause Chagas' disease and sleeping sickness are found over such a wide area and live in so many different insects that scientists are still unable to free millions of people from the great misery that these parasites can cause.

Life in the Mountains of Montana

Montana: Native Americans called it the Land of the Shining Mountains. Some 40 percent of the state is covered with mountains. There are the Big Belt and Little Belt Mountains, the Tobacco Root and the Absaraka Mountains. There are the Ruby Range and the Gallatin Range, the Madison Range and the Beartooth Range, and many others—all part of the Rocky Mountains, that spectacular chain of mountains that runs north to south across the North American continent.

Some of Montana's mountains are more than 10,000 feet high, with peaks that are covered with snow all year round. Most of the mountains are covered with forests filled with pines, firs, and other evergreens. Between the mountains, where the land is lower, there are lush valleys, cut by rapidly flowing streams.

In view of Little Chief Mountain in Glacier National Park, Montana, a **chipmunk** may sleep away the winter in a snug burrow while an **elk** must remain active in order to survive.

The forests and meadows support a diverse community of animals. Each of the animals has its own unique adaptations for survival in this environment. Yet broad similarities are apparent.

One of the main features of this environment is the long winters. For months the land is covered with many feet of snow. All the animals that spend the winter in the Montana mountains have some way of surviving during this period of cold. Some birds and large mammals can remain active throughout the winter. For them, the search for food must go on. Deer nibble on barren branches. Elk strip and eat the bark of trees. For these animals, and for the antelopes, the search for food is often unsuccessful; winter can be a time of near starvation.

Predators such as the mountain lion roam the snowy land. The mountain lion watches a herd of deer, hoping to get near enough to attack. If it can bring down a deer, it will eat seven to eight pounds of meat. The rest of the deer's body will be left in the snow—but not for long. Coyotes will find it and strip the bones of all remaining meat. Such leftovers form a major part of the coyote's diet, especially in winter. But the coyote also is a predator. It is particularly fond of sheep, a trait that has earned it the anger of Montana's sheep ranchers.

Other animals, such as ground squirrels, chipmunks, and marmots, spend the winter months in underground burrows or in caves. Here they enter hibernation, a condition in which their body temperature drops, their blood pressure falls, and their heartbeat and breathing rates slow down. The energy needed by their bodies during hibernation is not great. It is obtained by burning fat that they had built up during the previous summer and fall.

To pass through the cold months, the black bear enters a deep sleep. This is similar to hibernation except that the bear's body temperature does not drop, and its bodily functions continue at normal levels. Occasionally it may wake up and leave its winter home, or den—especially if there is a warm spell and melting snow floods the den.

If the female bear is pregnant, she will give birth during this time. Usually, a litter consists of two cubs. They are hairless, blind, and very small—no larger than a guinea pig. For the first month or so of their lives the cubs can nurse without even waking their mother.

Tree squirrels also do not hibernate. They live on food gathered in the fall. They must periodically leave their homes to reach their food supplies, which are buried nearby under the snow. As a tree squirrel moves across the snow, it is easy prey for predators. A marten, noticing the small animal, stalks it until it is near enough to attack. If the tree squirrel realizes the danger in time, it may escape by scampering back to its home. Otherwise, it becomes a meal for the marten.

The bears leave their dens about the time that the streams are finally free of ice. This is a sure sign of spring. So are the flowers that have blanketed the meadows and the birds that have returned after wintering in the south.

Mountain lions are the swiftest predators in the Montana mountains. Often **coyotes**, fighting among themselves, will finish eating the prey brought down by a mountain lion after the lion has eaten its fill.

The baby bears are about eight weeks old when they first see the outside world. They stay close to their mother, who keeps a watchful eye on them at all times. If a cub strays from its mother, it may become an easy victim for a mountain lion.

The young bears stay with their mother for two years. During this time, the mother teaches them how to protect themselves, find and catch food, and other skills needed to survive. One of the first things she teaches the cubs is to obey her. Discipline is an important part of the relationship between a mother bear and her cubs. She expects the youngsters to follow her commands. A cub who misbehaves soon gets a swat on its rear end that sends it flying through the air.

One of the first skills learned by the cubs is how to climb a tree. At first the cubs' climbing attempts are clumsy, and they fall off. But they soon perfect their tree-climbing talents. In fact, a black bear can climb a tree almost as quickly as a squirrel.

The cubs learn that they are to climb a tree only when their mother allows them to. If a curious cub decides on its own that a tree looks particularly inviting and starts to scramble up it, the mother will pull the cub down. There is a good reason for this parental discipline. Up in the tree may be one of the cub's worst enemies: an adult male bear. He will attack and kill an unprotected cub.

A black bear may look clumsy, but it is a fast and skillful climber.

Sometimes a female bear will send her cubs up a tree for more selfish reasons—she may wish to be rid of them for a while and wander through the forest by herself, to enjoy a quiet meal.

Bears eat a wide variety of plant and animal matter, including leaves, roots, fruit, acorns, insects, fish, and mice. They will turn over a rotting log or a stone in search of such tasty tidbits as grubs and ants. They will chase and kill young deer, antelope, and moose. If they live near people, they will raid garbage cans, apple orchards, and pig pens. Bears also climb trees to reach beehives from which they steal honey. The bees protest by trying to sting the bears. But a bear's thick fur coat protects it from the stings. About the only vulnerable part of the bear is its nose, and even there a bee sting feels like little more than a pin prick.

Spring is the season during which young animals are most plentiful in the Montana mountains. Some, such as the bear, coyote, and porcupine young, were born in winter dens. Others, such as the deer young, were born in spring. So were the young birds whose parents had wintered in the south.

For many of these young animals, learning is a game—at least part of the time. A young porcupine

A porcupine has as many as 30,000 loosely attached quills on its body. If a predator gets caught in the quills they are difficult to remove because each quill has barbs on the end.

92

practices swinging itself up onto a branch. A group of coyote pups play tag, chasing each other round and round. Each snaps at the tail of the pup in front of it. Elk calves play tag and have butting contests. Bear cubs also enjoy a game of tag, which often ends up as a wrestling match. Or the cubs may playfully fight over a stick.

Being curious as well as playful, bear cubs may try to play with some of the other inhabitants of the area. This can have unpleasant results. A skunk may react to a cub's advances by turning around and firing off a repulsive-smelling spray. If the skunk hits its target, the unfortunate bear will walk around for days smelling terrible.

A worse fate may be in store for a cub who bothers a porcupine. The bear may end up with a face full of quills. If these cannot be removed by the cub, its mouth may swell up so much that it will be unable to eat and so will slowly starve to death.

As temperatures increase, the snowline recedes higher and higher into the mountains. Herds of elk, which wintered in the forests, follow the receding snowline. They will spend the summer in high secluded meadows. Plentiful supplies of grass will fill out the stomachs that shrank during the lean winter months. The males, who shed their antlers in late winter, will grow new ones. By August, a mature male

Black bears are thought of as being ferocious. But a mother bear is tender with her cubs, and even a lone adult can relax on a warm day.

This black bear knew when the brook trout were running, so he caught himself a fine dinner.

for instance, stand on their hind legs and strike one another with savage blows. Most of the blows land on the opponent's head and shoulders and aren't very painful. But a blow that hits the stomach—or a bite in the arm—brings cries of pain. Eventually it becomes obvious that one bear is winning. The loser, sensing this, tries to break free and run off.

The winner and the female show much affection for one another. They hug and nuzzle each other, playfully wrestle, and wander side by side through the forest. This affection, however, does not last long. Soon after mating the two bears part and go their separate ways.

Black bears are predominately solitary creatures. They also are shy and will move away from, rather than toward, trouble. But if cornered or angry, the bear can be a fiercesome opponent. One animal it avoids is its large relative, the grizzly bear. If these two animals are present in the same area, the black bear will wander about and do much of its feeding during the day, since the grizzly usually rests during the day and wanders about in the evening.

As summer ends, one of the bear's favorite foods becomes available: berries. The bears spend many hours ripping juicy berries from bushes and stuffing them into their mouths. Many of the berries fall to the ground, where chipmunks and mice are ready to grab them.

Autumn brings cooler weather to the Montana mountains. Days shorten and storm clouds gather overhead. The animals begin to prepare for winter. Tree squirrels build up a supply of pine cones. Ground squirrels are busy fattening themselves on clover and various grasses that have grown tall in the summer sun. And the yellow-bellied marmot gathers and stores hay and roots. All of these animals also devote time to getting their homes in shape for the winter period of inactivity.

Ducks, geese, and many of the other birds that summered in Montana gather in large flocks and prepare to fly south to warmer areas. The elk gradually descend from the high mountains. They travel in long, ragged lines, following trails used year after year. Often, the males and females form separate groups and spend the winter apart.

As the first blizzard of winter blankets the mountains with snow, the bears begin to search for a comfortable den. The dens chosen by black bears vary greatly. They may be a hollow log or a cave. They may be a bed of moss beneath the low-hanging branches of a tree or a hollow beneath a rock ledge. The animals, armed with a thick layer of fat, settle into their dens and fall asleep.

will have a magnificent pair of antlers that may be five feet long and weigh as much as 50 pounds.

For elk and many other animals, midsummer brings the onset of the mating season. Fish swim upstream to lay their eggs. Many never complete the journey, for the bears are waiting. With their big paws, they flip the fish out of the water and onto the riverbank.

The female bear with young cubs has no interest in mating. She only mates every other summer, when her offspring from the previous mating are almost two years old. Then she must leave her cubs. She may do this by sending them up a tree, then walking away. The well-trained youngsters wait patiently for her return. They may stay in the trees for several days, confused by her long absence but still waiting for her to tell them it is all right to come down. Eventually, however, hunger overcomes discipline, and the bears climb down from the tree. They now are on their own.

Often there are fierce battles between two males who are rivals for the same female. Male bears,

A Cave Where Crickets Reign

Rainwater soaks into the ground. It dissolves some of the rocks and carries them away. Slowly, over many thousands of years, if conditions are right, a cave is formed.

Like any new environment, the cave does not remain unpopulated for long. Perhaps a flood deposits fish or worms in the cave. Water seeping down from the surface may carry algae or bacteria. A snail or beetle may wander in.

If the new environment provides conditions suitable for a plant or animal, it will stay. Free, at least momentarily, of the competitors and predators in its former environment, it may flourish in the new environment. Some of the members of the population will be better adapted to the new environment than others. They will live longer and produce more offspring, thereby passing on their special adaptations. In time, the population may be very different in structure and behavior from the plants or animals that first settled the new habitat.

This is the case with Cathedral Cave, one of the smaller caves in Mammoth Cave National Park, an extensive cave system located in Kentucky. One of the best and most interesting studies of cave life was conducted in Cathedral Cave in the 1960's by Christian Brother G. Nicholas, a biologist at La Salle College in Philadelphia. His study added greatly to our understanding of the food chains and interdependencies among members of a community.

With the help of several assistants, Nicholas divided the cave into 12 sections. Any invertebrate (animal without a backbone) found in the cave was marked and its position was noted. The animal was marked with a spot of harmless paint. A different color of paint was used for each of the 12 sections. Thus a cricket found in one section was marked with red paint while a cricket found in another section was marked with blue paint. This procedure helped the scientists learn the home territories of the animals and keep track of how far each animal wandered.

Every day for three years Nicholas or one of his assistants visited Cathedral Cave. Every day the researchers would note the position of every animal and mark any that had not previously been seen and painted.

In the depths of the cave there is no light. Animals that do not come out into the sunlight are called troglodytes (TROG-la-dites). Most are eyeless. And most are colorless. This lack of pigment makes them prisoners in their dark world. Even a few seconds of exposure to sunlight would kill them.

Among the animals tracked by the researchers were flatworms, earthworms, snails, small crustaceans

Mammoth Cave National Park, established in 1941, contains 12 miles of underground corridors open to visitors accompanied by guides.

The common cave cricket has long legs and
antennae that make it look somewhat like a
spider. It is nearly blind and does not chirp.

called isopods and amphipods, spiders, millipedes,
harvestmen, and beetles. But the most numerous
species was the common cave cricket *Hadenoecus
subterraneus*. This pale brown insect has long legs
and very long antennae. Its eyes are small and its
eyesight poor in comparison to that of its surface
relatives. And unlike surface-dwelling crickets, *H.
subterraneus* is silent. It does not chirp.

The researchers found that some animals lived
on the ceiling of the cave while others were found
almost solely on either the walls or the floor. The
crickets, for example, were always found hanging
from the ceiling. Harvestmen, cave spiders, millipedes, and snails lived on the walls. Amphipods and
isopods swam about in streams or pools of water on
the floor. These white, eyeless creatures were attacked and eaten by the flatworms. As the flatworms
moved across the bottoms of streams, they left behind trails of mucus. An unwary isopod that stepped
into this sticky secretion would be unable to free
itself. Trapped, it would lie there helplessly.
Eventually, a worm came along and ate it.

Small, blind beetles lived in muddy areas of the
floor. They fed on bacteria that grew on the mud.
Other beetles were scavengers that fed on the bodies
of dead crickets and other animals. If they over-
looked a dead body, mold soon formed on it and it
became food for still other creatures.

A spot of color was provided by the cave
salamanders. They were bright orange with black
spots. They scampered over floor, walls, and ceiling,
eating almost any animal they could catch. One of
their favorite foods in winter were mosquitoes that
had moved into the cave to escape the cold weather.

Most of the members of Cathedral Cave did not
wander very far. Nicholas and his assistants always
found the great majority of the animals in the same
section of the cave in which they originally were
marked.

In fact, the Nicholas project proved that the
only inhabitants that left the cave were crickets.
Crickets are plant-eaters. Because of the lack of light,
green plants cannot live in a cave. Therefore, the
crickets had to go on feeding expeditions into the
outside world. Every night, as darkness fell, one-third
of the cricket colony would leave the cave. They
would stay outdoors all night, feeding. Before sun-
rise, they returned to the cave, each to its proper section of the ceiling. The next night, another third of
the cricket colony went outdoors to feed. And on the
third night, the remaining group went outdoors. This
three-night cycle was repeated over and over again.

The crickets were the cave's only important
source of plant food. Because of this, they were at the
base of the cave's food chain. Some of the other
inhabitants, such as the salamander, fed directly on

The cave salamander (above) is one of the few brightly colored cave dwellers.

This cave-dwelling spider (right) is sightless.

the crickets. Others fed on or laid their eggs on the wastes excreted by the crickets. These animals in turn were eaten by still other animals. Thus directly or indirectly all the cave-dwelling animals benefited from the crickets' outside food-gathering.

There were 3,750 crickets living in Cathedral Cave at the time of the Nicholas investigation. The total of all the other animals in the cave was much lower. It was a small community, made up of small animals. But it functioned exactly the same way as any large community in the open air.

The word "millipede" means 1,000 legs, but no millipede actually has a thousand legs.

Confronting a Changing World

Once, vast marshes bordered Newark Bay and the Hackensack River in northeastern New Jersey. The marshes were home for a wide variety of wildlife. Herring gulls, mallards, and clapper rails bred there. So did the snowy egret, one of the most beautiful birds. The waters were an important spawning, nursery, and feeding ground for young fish. The intertidal areas were home to clams, barnacles, snails, and fiddler crabs. Sandpipers dashed along the intertidal area, picking up the tiny animals as they were exposed by the receding tides. Mallards, sanderlings, and black-and-white ducks called scaups also fed on these animals. Snapping turtles prowled in search of frogs and baby ducks. Mosquitoes bred here; their young served as food for various birds and fish.

In the late summer swallows, bobolinks, and tens of thousands of other migrating birds visited the marshes. The marshes were directly under the Atlantic Flyway, the major route for bird migration in eastern North America. The marshes were a pleasant resting spot for the birds, who stayed perhaps a week or more before continuing their journey southward. These birds visited the area again in the spring as they made the return journey to the north.

Gradually, however, the environment of the marsh changed. Factories were built along the Hackensack River. They dumped their wastes into the river. Towns also dumped wastes, including sewage, into the river. This polluted the water and led to the death of fish and intertidal animals. As the populations of these animals decreased, there was less food for the birds.

An airport was built nearby. The noise of low-flying planes frightened the birds. Some of the birds abandoned their eggs, thereby dooming the young before they were even hatched.

Developers came. More and more of the marsh was filled in. Roads and houses and office buildings and a large sports stadium were built. No longer was there room for thousands of migrating birds. No longer were there nesting sites for great blue herons. No longer was there enough wildlife to support predators such as the marsh hawk.

A small portion of these marshes has been saved.

Snow geese by the thousands stop in the New Jersey salt marshes on their migration journeys.

Marshlands can be destroyed by industrial development (left) that pollutes the waters or by filling in the land for a garbage dump (above) and, eventually, more development.

But most is gone. What has happened to the animals that lived here?

Some have adapted. The herring gull has thrived, for it seems to be just as content to feed on people's garbage as on insects and the eggs of other birds. Mallards also have adapted. They are willing to live in small parks and other small open areas.

In most cases, however, the populations of the marsh animals have dropped drastically. The environment has been reshaped for the convenience and use of people. The needs of wildlife conflict with the needs of the "modern world."

Such changes are occurring all over the world. Habitats of one kind are being replaced by different habitats. Many factors are responsible for these changes.

Sometimes the changes are caused by shifts in weather patterns. The most dramatic example of this was the great Ice Age, which began almost a million years ago. For reasons still unknown to us, large glaciers drifted southward from the Arctic ice cap.

The glaciers brought cold weather. Eventually, large masses of ice blanketed much of North America, Europe, and Asia. At their greatest extent, the glaciers reached as far south as New York, Ohio, and Missouri. For thousands of years, the ice advanced and retreated. The weight of the ice crushed the underlying earth, forming basins and valleys. The levels of the sea fell because so much water remained frozen on land, then rose when the ice finally melted. Many animals adapted to warmer climates became extinct. Others moved, thus causing great changes in the distribution of species.

Earthquakes and volcanic eruptions can change environments. In 1963, the eruption of an underwater volcano off the southern coast of Iceland created a new island. By the time the volcano stopped spewing forth molten rock the island, named Surtsey, had grown to an area of about one square mile. It replaced an equal area of sea, meaning that the fish that had swum there now had to swim elsewhere. But it wasn't long before birds flew to the island. Some left behind droppings that contained undigested plant seeds. Two years after Surtsey was formed, it had its first plant. Today it is home for a variety of living things.

Many changes in an environment are caused by animals themselves. Animals can change the kinds and amount of vegetation and have an impact on the physical structure of the land. One of the best examples of this is found in the extraordinary dam building of the beaver. Beavers can build huge dams. One dam at Three Forks, Montana, is 2,140 feet long!

A beaver dam, made of rocks, branches, mud and weeds, protects the beaver by creating a shallow pond that hides the entrance to the beavers' home. But at the same time, the new pond drowns the life that had lived on the land. By cutting down trees and digging canals, the beavers also destroy habitats of land animals. On the positive side, the pond helps ensure a steady supply of drinking water for wildlife during dry summer months, it provides a nesting area for waterfowl, and it provides a home for fish and other freshwater animals that need a quiet place in which to live.

A change in an environment that results in one community being replaced by another community is called succession. The replacement of a stream by a beaver pond is an example of succession. So is the replacement of a marsh by a community of people.

The first people, who lived perhaps one million years ago, were as much at the mercy of the Ice Age and other natural changes as any other animal. They dug for roots, gathered berries, hunted animals. They lived from day to day. If the winters were extremely severe, they died of the cold. If a prolonged drought occurred and game was scarce, they died of starvation.

Gradually, though, people took more and more control. They used their superior intelligence to change the world to suit their needs. They discovered how to control fire. They discovered how to farm plants and domesticate animals. They learned how to mine the earth's resources and how to melt and cast metals. They built towns and roads, factories powered by huge machines, automobiles, and airports. They developed chemicals to rid their homes and crops of insect pests. Each of these and many thousands of other developments has had its effect on the environment . . . and on wildlife.

Sometimes the introduction of a new animal into an environment can cause changes. Such an animal (or plant) is called an exotic. Although the introduction of exotics may be considered an asset, more often than not they cause more harm than good. They upset the delicate balance that exists in an environment. As a result, they often pose threats to animals native to the environment.

In some cases, the introduction of an exotic is accidental. Rodents that stow away on a ship in one port may disembark at a port on another continent halfway around the world. Insect eggs may travel on fruit as it is sent from one place to another.

In other cases, the introduction of an exotic is deliberate. Wild African bees were imported to Brazil in 1956 in hopes that they would interbreed with local bees, creating a better honey producer. A few months later, 26 swarms of the African bees escaped from their hives. Because they were hardier and more aggressive than local bees, they rapidly intermixed with the local bees in many areas and earned the nickname "killer bees." The African bees soon enlarged their range, moving northward through South America and into Central America. In ten years they may reach the United States. How they will affect bees now living in North America is still not known.

A black-crowned night heron sits on a barrel in what once may have been ideal breeding or feeding grounds. Now, pollution may threaten the heron's very existence.

101

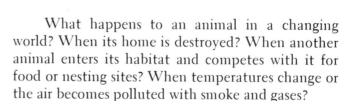

The white-tailed kite manages to survive and even to breed in the low brush surrounding the busy California freeways.

The Alaska pipeline drops underground in some places to allow the free passage of animals. **An Arctic fox** has found temporary refuge in a pipe stored for emergency repairs.

What happens to an animal in a changing world? When its home is destroyed? When another animal enters its habitat and competes with it for food or nesting sites? When temperatures change or the air becomes polluted with smoke and gases?

Some animals adapt to the changes. For example, the white-tailed kite of California once lived in grasslands and marshes. As these were turned into farmland, the kite population dropped greatly. The bird seemed headed for extinction. But then it found itself a new home—the California freeways. It learned to feed on the many insects and mice that live along the edge of the freeways and in the median strips that divide the opposing lanes of traffic. The kite also found that these areas provided relatively safe nesting sites.

In Alaska, a recent major change has been the tapping of the oil reserves in Prudhoe Bay and the construction of a 1,300-mile pipeline from Prudhoe Bay southward to the Gulf of Alaska. How is wildlife adjusting to these changes? It is still too soon to fully answer this question. However, there already are signs of new behavior. For example, some Arctic foxes now prowl among the Prudhoe Bay settlements and feed on garbage. Their bellies full, they don't have to hunt for prey. Thus, the populations of voles and other animals on which the foxes naturally prey may increase. Or the population of another predator may increase, since it no longer has as much competition from the foxes.

The white-tailed kite and the Arctic fox are examples of animals that have adapted to changes by changing their behavior. Some animals adapt by changing the way they look. An excellent example of this is some 100 species of English moths. Originally, these moths were light-colored. This was a fine protective adaptation because the moths spent much of their time on tree trunks covered with light-colored lichens (moss-like plants). But as parts of England became industrialized, the air became filled with black smoke. Soot from the factories settled on the trees, turning them dark. Life became more difficult for the moths. When they rested on a tree, their light color no longer blended in. Instead, it stood out against the blackened tree trunk. Birds easily spotted the moths and swooped down to eat them.

In any species, there is some variety in appearance. This is as true with moths as it is with people. Although most of these English moths were light-colored, some members of each species were darker. This had previously been a disadvantage. But with the darkened trees, it became an advantage. It hid the moths from the birds. Thus the dark-colored moths began to have a better chance of surviving than did their light-colored relatives. This meant they had a better chance to reproduce and pass on their dark appearance to their offspring.

Gradually, dark-colored moths replaced light-colored moths in each of the species of moths. An intriguing question can now be posed: What happens to the dark-colored moths as pollution controls begin to clean up the English air? The light-colored forms may once again predominate.

Some animals adapt to changes in their environment by leaving. They move elsewhere. This may, in turn, displace other animals.

Finally, there are animals that cannot adapt to changes in their environment. And so they die. This is most apt to happen if the population is small and is found in a limited area. For example, in the 1950s, builders near Tecopa, California, rechanneled some hot water springs that were home for the Tecopa pupfish. This 1½-inch-long fish, which required salty water and warm temperatures, lived in the springs and adjoining small pools. The rechanneling created a swiftly flowing river, which greatly restricted the pupfish's habitat. Later, mosquito fish were introduced into the river to eat mosquitoes. But the mosquito fish also fed on young pupfish, further reducing the pupfish population. The last Tecopa pupfish was seen in 1970. In 1978 the Tecopa pupfish was removed from the list of endangered species—the first animal to be removed because it no longer existed.

This final chapter looks at how different animals have confronted a changing world. The first section illustrates how a human "improvement" can upset the natural balance in an environment, creating far more problems than it solves. The next two sections show what can happen when animals are brought into a new environment. The concluding section explores the continuing problem of endangered animals.

These two moths illustrate how one is better adapted to an environment that is dingy and sooty than is the other.

Why Cats Were Parachuted onto Borneo

At the western end of the Pacific Ocean north of Australia lies a large island named Borneo. It is a tropical land where days and nights are always warm.

Borneo receives so much rain that people say it has two seasons, a rainy season and a less rainy season. As a result of all the rain, there are many swampy areas on Borneo. These are an ideal environment for crocodiles. They also are ideal for an even deadlier animal: the mosquito.

For centuries the people of Borneo died at early ages from malaria, a disease spread by the *Anopheles* (a-NOF-a-leez) mosquito. The disease is caused by a protozoan that lives in the saliva of the mosquito. When the mosquito bites a person, its saliva mixes with the person's blood and the protozoan enters the person's body.

While some scientists tried to develop drugs that would prevent people from getting malaria or that would cure those who were infected, other scientists worked on ways to kill the mosquitoes that carried the malaria. In 1939, a Swiss scientist, Paul Hermann Müller, discovered that a chemical known for more than 60 years would kill insects. The chemical was dichloro-diphenyl-trichloroethane. The world knows it as DDT.

After World War II, DDT began to be widely used in tropical areas where malaria was common. It was sprayed over wide areas of Borneo—over forests and fields, swamps and rivers, homes and schools. It was sprayed inside homes, too, on the walls, ceilings, and floors. The DDT was absorbed by the malaria-carrying mosquitoes and killed them. The amount of malaria on Borneo dropped sharply. The people began to live longer, more productive lives.

And that seemed to be the end of the story. However, it was only the beginning.

The DDT was absorbed not only by mosquitoes but also by many other animals (and plants) on Borneo. It was absorbed by cockroaches. But it didn't kill the cockroaches. What killed the cockroaches was the same enemy that always had killed cockroaches on Borneo: long-tailed lizards called geckos.

The people of Borneo loved the geckos and happily shared their homes with these little creatures. The geckos would scamper up and down the walls of the houses, across the thatched roofs, and across the floors in search of cockroaches and other insects.

When a gecko ate a cockroach that had absorbed DDT, the DDT passed into the gecko's body. The more cockroaches a gecko ate, the greater amount of DDT that concentrated in its body. The DDT concentrated in the nervous system of the gecko and it affected the lizard's behavior. The lizard's movements became slower. The animal became less alert.

Another animal loved by the people of Borneo was the cat. Cats took care of another pest. They caught and ate rats. The cats rarely caught geckos, for the lizards moved much too quickly. But the DDT-filled geckos were different. They were easy to catch. So the cats caught and ate the lizards. As a result, the DDT began to concentrate in their bodies. And it affected them just as it had the geckos and the mosquitoes. The cats became sluggish and, gradually, they died.

Village life in Borneo has been effected by modern improvements, but the basic patterns of life remain much as they have existed for centuries.

The people of Borneo were saddened by the loss of their pets. But there was worse to come. With the cats gone, the rat population increased greatly. More and more rats were seen around the people's houses. The people became frantic, for they knew that rats carry bubonic plague—a disease more dreadful than malaria. Something had to be done. Fast.

A large number of cats was flown to Borneo and parachuted down to the villages. The cats quickly caught a lot of rats and chased others back into the forests.

The people were just beginning to breathe sighs of relief when another calamity hit them. The thatched roofs of their homes began collapsing. Again, DDT was to blame. In addition to eating cockroaches, the geckos ate caterpillars that lived in —and ate—the thatched roof. While the geckos were alive, the caterpillar population was kept under control and damage to the roofs was slight. But with the geckos gone, the caterpillars thrived and multiplied.

A domestic cat, no matter where in the world it lives, retains its hunting instinct. In Borneo, as in many other places, it hunts rats.

Thus a program begun to rid Borneo of mosquitoes had both positive and negative results. The mosquitoes were controlled, but at an unexpected cost.

In the years since DDT was first used to control insects, scientists have learned a great deal about the interrelationships in the animal world. They have learned that attempts to interfere with or to change the environmental balance—the ecology of an area—can have unforeseen consequences—consequences that can harm people as well as wildlife.

The gecko can walk up, down, across, or even upside down because of the suction disks on the bottom of each of its broad toes.

105

Naturalized Citizens: House Sparrows and Starlings

At one time, house sparrows (members of the weaver finch family) lived only in Europe, North Africa, and parts of Asia. Starlings lived only in Europe. Today these birds, especially house sparrows, are found around the world. They have gone not only to North America but also to Australia, New Zealand, southern Africa, and many places in between.

House sparrows and starlings were introduced to these new homes by people. The birds were introduced primarily because people thought they would control insect pests.

Both birds entered North America through the same port: New York City. The English, or house, sparrow came first. People hoped it would attack the cankerworm, an insect that was causing much damage to shade trees. Several pairs of house sparrows were introduced in the fall of 1850, but they apparently died. In 1853 more house sparrows were brought over. Many of these survived and soon began to breed, thereby increasing the population.

In the following years, many hundreds of house sparrows were imported and released in the northeastern United States. Texas, Illinois, and other states in the central part of the country also received birds for release. In 1871 the house sparrow was introduced to California. Everywhere, this bird thrived and extended its range.

The successful adjustment of the house sparrows to life in the United States was due to several factors. First, it is a hardy animal. It can survive year round in temperature climates that include hot summers and icy winters. It makes its home in a wide variety of habitats—cities, suburbs, farming areas. Second, it has a high birth rate. A female nests at least twice a year and may nest 4 or even 5 times. Each brood contains 4 to 7 fledglings, all of which usually survive.

Third, the house sparrow is an aggressive animal. It will take over the nesting sites of barn swallows, house wrens, and other birds. It may even destroy these birds' eggs. It monopolizes food supplies, driving off other birds that try to feed.

Fourth, in North America house sparrows have few natural enemies, although cats, hawks, and owls

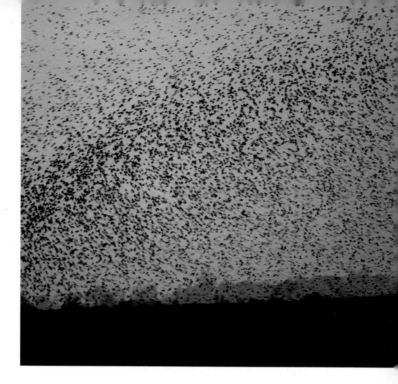

A flock of starlings nearly blackens the sky.

Starlings (middle) and house sparrows (bottom) have adapted themselves to all kinds of places to roost and to make their nests.

do prey on them and today many are killed by automobiles.

Fifth, house sparrows eat a wide variety of food. Their diet, as Americans eventually learned, is not limited to insects considered harmful. In fact, when investigators killed some house sparrows and analyzed the contents of their stomachs, they found that relatively few of the birds ate insects. And those that did eat insects ate as many helpful insects as harmful ones. As a matter of fact, the house sparrow's primary food is seed—the seeds of weeds, of recently sown gardens, of maturing wheat crops, and so on. They also eat grapes, cherries, and other fruits. They eat buds, flowers, and the tender stalks of young vegetables. In cities they feed largely on garbage.

It is estimated that in one day 50 house sparrows eat the equivalent of a quart of wheat. Imagine, then, how much food is needed by the millions of house sparrows that now live in the United States.

Finally, when house sparrows were first introduced into the United States, people did what they could to encourage the bird's survival. In most states, laws were passed to protect house sparrows. In Boston, when the great northern shrike began preying on house sparrows, the city hired someone to shoot the shrikes.

However, by the 1880s people realized that the importation of house sparrows had brought, at best, mixed blessings. States began to repeal the protective laws. In their place, some states passed laws designed to eliminate the house sparrows. For example, in 1883 Pennsylvania passed this law: "Be it enacted that . . . it shall be lawful at any season of the year to kill or in any way destroy the small bird known as the English sparrow." Michigan went a step further in 1887, when it offered a 1-cent bounty for each dead house sparrow.

Such laws, however, did not work. There were too many house sparrows and they were too well adapted to be controlled.

The history of starlings followed a similar pattern. The first 80 birds were released in New York City's Central Park on March 6, 1890, by Eugene Scheifflin, who thought it would be nice to import into the United States all the birds mentioned in the works of William Shakespeare. In the spring of 1891, 40 more starlings were released. Some of the birds stayed in or near the park. Others flew off and settled in other parts of the city. Gradually they spread throughout New York State and into neighboring states.

As with the house sparrow, the starling population grew rapidly. The starling is a very hardy and

House sparrows like many other birds, are fond of berries, but they also eat valuable seed crops.

intelligent bird, well adapted for the battle of life. It usually reproduces twice a year, with 3 to 6 young in each brood.

The starling will eat a variety of foods, but prefers insects and fruits. There is no doubt that the starling is a very effective predator of grasshoppers and other insect pests. The problem is that the starling also ruins crops such as cherries and grapes.

Like house sparrows, starlings compete with other birds for nesting sites—and usually win. As a region's starling population increased, the populations of such native birds as flickers, bluebirds, and martins decreased.

Both house sparrows and starlings are gregarious (gra-GAR-ee-us) birds. That is, they gather together in large groups. A flock of hundreds of house sparrows or starlings descending on a strawberry field can cause great damage. In cities they gather in parks, on the ledges of buildings, and in other sheltered spots. They are not the cleanest of animals. Their droppings deface buildings, mess sidewalks, and damage, even kill, trees and other plants. The birds can be dangerous in the air, too. For example, in 1960 a flock of starlings had a head-on collision with an airplane. The plane crashed, killing 62 people.

For North Americans and other people who share their environment with these birds, the benefits of house sparrows and starlings are offset by the damage they cause. The people who supported the importing of the birds thought only of the possible benefits. By the time people realized the high environmental cost of introducing the birds, it was too late. They were here to stay.

Here Comes the African Clawed Frog

It has a flat, pear-shaped body, a narrow head, and tiny round eyes. Its front limbs are small and stick out at right angles to its body. Its hind limbs are huge and end in large webbed feet.

It's the African clawed frog, one of the most unusual looking of the highly aquatic frogs. The three inner toes of each rear foot end in hard, sharp claws—giving the frog its name. The webbing extends to the tip of the toes. When the webbing and toes are spread wide, the foot's width is almost one-half the length of the frog's body. Such well-developed legs and feet make the African clawed frog a powerful swimmer. Unlike most frogs, it can swim backward as well as forward. This is very useful in escaping from predators.

Another defensive mechanism is the frog's ability to change color. When the frog is on a dark background it is a dark olive gray. If it moves to a light background or if the amount of sunlight hitting it increases, it can change to a light brown or beige. It also can change its pattern, becoming either solid colored or spotted.

The African clawed frog lives in fresh water, feeding and breeding underwater. It may stay underwater for long periods of time before moving to the surface to breathe. If the pond in which it lives

African clawed frogs swim through **drainage pipes** to new locations, ever broadening their range.

The African clawed frog can use its large webbed and clawed feet to swim forward or backward, giving it an advantage over other frogs.

dries up, the frog may bury itself in the mud, remaining there until rain once again fills the pond. Or it may travel overland to another pond. It can do this, however, only when it is rainy or very humid—or if there is a connecting marsh. The frog's skin must be kept damp. If it dries out, the frog will die.

The frog also may move to new quarters if the pond in which it is living becomes overpopulated. These frogs increase their numbers at a rapid rate. The breeding season begins in early spring and lasts four to five months. In that time, a female usually lays 10,000 eggs—and may lay as many as 15,000. The eggs hatch in two or three days.

The young tadpoles feed on mosquito larvae and other tiny animals. The adults seem to eat almost anything that moves—the larvae of mosquitoes and other insects, eggs, worms, tiny crustaceans and fish, even frogs almost as big as they are. Sometimes they scavenge.

The frog has an excellent sense of smell and depends on it for finding food. Once it has detected food, it will wave its front legs about in a clapping motion, until it locates the food. The front feet grasp the food and push it into the animal's mouth.

In southern Africa, its natural home, the African clawed frog lives in balance with other creatures. But in southern California, its new home, its killing off all sorts of native animals. How did it travel halfway round the world?

The first African clawed frogs arrived in the United States in the 1940s, after medical scientists discovered that the frogs could be used to determine if a woman is pregnant. The urine of a pregnant woman contains hormones not found in the urine of a woman who isn't pregnant. When the urine of a pregnant woman is injected into a female African clawed frog, the frog will lay eggs within 24 hours. The urine of a woman who isn't pregnant produces no response.

The use of frogs for pregnancy testing was eventually replaced by other simpler and more reliable tests. But other laboratory uses of the frogs continued. They have, for instance, been used by scientists to study the structure and reproduction of cells. Unlike most other common frogs, the African clawed frog is easy to keep and breed under laboratory conditions.

Some of the frogs, however, left the world of microscopes and test tubes. They were taken home by people who thought they would make interesting pets. Some escaped—those powerful hind legs enable the frogs to easily jump out of an aquarium. Others were probably put outdoors by owners after the frogs began eating tropical fish kept in the same aquarium.

In the late 1960s biologists began finding the frogs in drainage channels and ponds in various parts of southern California. Every year that passed brought reports of their presence in new places ... and reports that other wildlife in those habitats were disappearing. The populations of tree frogs, aquatic frogs, and western toads have declined. Biologists now fear that the African clawed frog will get into habitats of such endangered animals as the unarmored three-spined stickleback. If this happens, it will probably mean the end of the little fish.

African clawed frogs can adapt to a great variety of environmental conditions. They can live at sea level and at altitudes up to several thousand feet. They can survive well in water temperatures from 50 to 80° F. They can stand great increases in the salt content of the water.

Biologists in California put poison in some of the ponds where African clawed frogs had taken over. The frogs reacted by leaving the ponds and heading for other bodies of water. Trapping also has been unsuccessful. In fact, where biologists trapped some of the frogs, the population actually increased the following year: because there were fewer adult frogs, more tadpoles survived and grew to maturity.

Is it a losing battle? Will the three-spined stickleback and other native species of southern California have to give way to the African clawed frog? Or will people figure out a way to get rid of this invader? Only time will tell. But at present things seem to be on the side of the frog with the strange feet.

Green tree frogs and other less aggressive and adaptable frogs may be displaced by the African clawed frogs.

109

Endangered Animals

In the last century, passenger pigeons were the most numerous birds in the United States. Some flocks contained a billion or even two billion birds. They were a popular food, were fed to pigs, and were even used as fertilizer. People slaughtered them and shipped them by the carloads. Today, there are no passenger pigeons. The species is extinct. The last passenger pigeon died on September 1, 1914.

Another bird that was easy to shoot and tasty to eat was the heath hen. Once common throughout the northeastern United States, it too is extinct. The last heath hen on earth lived on Martha's Vineyard, an island south of Cape Cod, Massachusetts. It was last seen on March 11, 1932.

Plains buffalo, once threatened with extinction, are now protected by law and are increasing steadily in numbers.

The passenger pigeon is now extinct. We must imagine what it looked like from stuffed models.

Extinction is not new. It has always happened. But through the impact of people, the pace at which animals die out has quickened. Since 1600, about 40 mammal species and 94 bird species have become extinct. With each passing century, the number has increased. In this, the twentieth century, an average of one species or subspecies a year dies out, never to be seen again.

People who are working to save endangered animals believe that at least 10 percent of the world's animals are threatened. Most of these are tropical species, and many are species we do not even know about because they live in isolated areas. Since many tropical species live in very small areas, the destruction of a dozen acres of forest or jungle can result in extinction of several species. No one knows what such a loss might mean to the world. The naturalist Ernest Thompson Seton, in comparing the loss of animals to the destruction of books, once wrote: "each animal is in itself an inexhaustible volume of facts that man

The dodo, a flightless bird of the island of Mauritius, became extinct during the 1600s.

must have, to solve the problem of knowing himself. One by one, not always deliberately, these wonderful volumes have been destroyed, and the facts that might have been read in them have been lost."

Of the animals that are native to the United States, at least 194 are endangered. The list currently includes 29 mammals, 70 birds, 23 amphibians and reptiles, 40 fishes, 23 mollusks, 8 insects, and 1 crustacean. It probably also should include many smaller animals about which it is difficult to obtain population information. What has brought these animals so close to extinction? What has caused the extinction of other animals?

Overhunting has been responsible for the extinction or decline of many animal populations. The plains buffalo, which once roamed in huge herds across the plains of North America, is a well-known example. Early European explorers and settlers of the region wrote with amazement of the herds. In 1851, a man who had long lived on the plains related this scene: ". . . from bluff to bluff on the north and on the south and up the valley to the westward—as far as the eye could reach—the broad valley was literally blackened by a compact mass of buffalo, and not only this—the massive bluffs on both sides were covered by thousands and thousands that were still pouring down into the already crowded valley, and as far as the eye could reach, the living dark masses covered

the ground completely as a carpet covers the floor."

As the American west was settled by pioneers, the number of buffalo killed each year grew. With the expansion of railroads into the area, the slaughter reached gigantic proportions. Millions of buffalo were killed—sometimes for their meat or hides, sometimes for political reasons (politicians thought that by killing the buffalos they could get rid of the Indians who were dependent on them), sometimes for the sheer "sport" of killing large animals.

In 1883, the last major herd of buffalo was killed. Thereafter, only small stray groups existed in hard to reach areas. A census in 1899 counted only 541 plains buffalo. Fortunately, before the last of these magnificent creatures were killed, several reserves were set aside for buffalo and laws were passed to protect them. From the brink of extinction, the species slowly made a comeback. By the early 1970s, some 30,000 buffalo could be found on North American ranges.

Overhunting has also caused many of the world's whales to be placed on endangered animals lists. In greatest danger of extinction is the blue whale. Once it was common in all the oceans. But the invention of the harpoon gun, huge factory ships, and other technology that improved the efficiency of whaling enabled people to catch and kill these whales. In the 1930-1931 whaling season, 29,000 blue whales were caught—82 percent of all the whales caught that season. By the mid-1960s, the figure had dropped to less than 5 percent of the total catch, not because hunters sought other whales instead but because they didn't see blue whales anymore.

Finally, in 1966, laws were enacted to limit the killing of blue whales. Many scientists fear, however, that these restrictions came too late to save the blue whale. They worry that the population—now estimated at between 3,000 and 4,000—is so small and so widely scattered in the oceans that the whales will not find each other during mating season. If they do not mate, the species will die out.

Most countries now have laws that regulate hunting and fishing. But these are not completely successful, largely because of the lure of money. Tigers are protected in India. But a woodcutter who illegally kills a tiger can sell its hide on the black market for a sum equal to seven months' salary. Hunters in the United States' Rocky Mountains are legally allowed to kill about 300 bighorn sheep each year. But the actual number of bighorns killed is much higher. The lure: a person can get several thousand dollars for the head of a male bighorn with large curling horns.

Because **blue whales** travel great distances, they were hunted in many parts of the world.

A whaling station in western Australia where whales, such as these **sperm whales,** are butchered.

Whale meat is put up in cans in Japan and sold to foreign markets as a delicacy.

The Rocky Mountain bighorn sheep is hunted for its impressive horns.

Another black-market operation involves unusual pets. People will pay large sums of money for exotic tropical fish, rare birds, monkeys, and other animals. For example, a baby orangutan can be sold for hundreds of dollars. The easiest way to capture a baby is to find one with its mother, then shoot the mother. Thus every captured orangutan means one less female breeding in the wild.

Predators have frequently been at the receiving end of bullets, traps, poisons, and other human weapons. Many people hate predators. A farmer, for example, may hate foxes because the foxes raid his chicken coop. But the loss of a few chickens usually is more than balanced by the good done by foxes. They keep down the populations of mice, rabbits, woodchucks, and insects that cause a great deal of damage to farmland.

The Vancouver Island wolf, a type of timber wolf that lives on Vancouver Island, is a predator now on Canada's list of rare and endangered species. At one time many such wolves lived on the island. But extensive hunting and poisoning campaigns were conducted by trappers and people who lived on the island.

Another danger to wildlife is loss of habitat. As the human population grows, more forests are cleared, more marshes are drained and filled with soil, more bodies of water are polluted with chemicals or heat or other wastes. New dams may threaten the

An orangutan infant taken from its mother may die because it is deprived of her affection. Yet people will kill a mother orangutan in order to capture the infant.

existence of certain kinds of fish. New buildings may cover a bird's traditional nesting grounds. New highways may separate animals from their source of food.

Many animals cannot adjust to such changes. One that cannot is the orangutan. It probably is the most endangered of all the great apes. Fewer than 4,500 are believed to be living in the wild. Orangutans live in thick tropical jungles on the islands of Borneo and Sumatra. As the jungles are destroyed, so are the orangutans. Says Dr. John MacKinnon, an anthropologist who has studied these animals: "Wherever man has penetrated, the orang has vanished—hunted for the pot, caught for pets, or simply because his habitat is destroyed."

Although many endangered animals are killed for money, money can also be used to save animals. In many places, private groups and government agencies are buying up unspoiled land and preserving it in its natural state. On Borneo and Sumatra several orangutan reserves have been established. These are located within the natural habitat of the orangs. No logging or other human activities that destroy the land or disturb the orangutans are allowed.

In the 1970s the governments on Borneo and Sumatra began enforcing a law that makes it illegal to keep orangutans as pets. People who owned such pets before the ban was enforced had to take their pets to the reserves. There, zoologists care for the ex-pets and slowly teach them how to survive in the wilderness. When the scientists feel the animals have become adjusted to their new environment, they are turned loose.

In wilderness areas and research centers around the world, scientists are studying ways to save endangered animals. They are studying the life cycles of animals to better understand the animals' needs. They are studying the animals' mating and breeding habits. They are looking for ways to solve special problems, such as how to remove oil from sea birds caught in oil spills.

Efforts to raise animals in captivity, then release them into the wild are being tried. The government of Papua New Guinea funds special farms where rare butterflies and crocodiles are bred. Scientists from Mexico and the United States are trying to save the Atlantic ridley turtle by taking newly laid eggs from a nesting area on the east coast of Mexico and hatching the eggs at the well-protected Padre Island National Seashore in Texas. After hatching, the young are raised in captivity for a year before being released into the seas. The success or failure of the program won't be known until the matured turtles are ready to breed. If they return to Padre Island, the program succeeded.

There are success stories in the fight to save endangered animals. The whooping crane, an elegant bird that has become the symbol of the movement to save American wildlife, is slowly making a comeback. By the late 1970s, there were more than 120 birds—a very small population, but impressive when we realize that in the 1940s only 14 whooping cranes remained in the wild. Today, some of the young birds are hatched and raised by their natural parents in the wild. Others are hatched and raised in captivity, then released. Still others develop from eggs placed with foster parents. The foster parents, sandhill cranes, accept the eggs as their own, incubate them, then raise the young whooping cranes. It is hoped that these whoopers will eventually leave the sandhill cranes and form their own flock. Other help in saving whooping cranes has come from the preservation of nesting and wintering grounds and the enforcement of strict protective laws.

The peregrine falcon, almost doomed by the chemical insecticide DDT, also appears to be saved.

Whooping cranes are carefully protected at their winter home, the Aransas Wildlife Refuge on the Gulf Coast of Texas. Whooping cranes are in the greatest danger as they migrate between their winter and summer homes.

Much of the credit for this belongs to Thomas Cade of Cornell University. He has been hatching peregrine falcons in captivity, then releasing them to the wild. Well, maybe "the wild" isn't always the proper term. Some of them were released in Baltimore, Maryland. In 1978, one of these birds, a female named Scarlet, settled down on a building ledge 33 floors above the street. She laid three eggs—the first time in 20 years that a peregrine falcon in the eastern United States had done so in the wild. The eggs hadn't been fertilized, so Cade replaced them with six young peregrines that had been born in captivity. Scarlet accepted them as her own and proceeded to care for them.

Although **peregrine falcons** are widely distributed around the world, exposure to DDT has lowered their fertility rate and breeding. It may take several generations to overcome the damage done by DDT.

An Atlantic ridley turtle is helpless against predators as it slowly crawls across the beach toward the water after laying her eggs. The journey is even more dangerous for the hatchlings. Polluted waters add a new threat to the Atlantic ridley's survival.

Peregrine falcons may be able to adjust to city living throughout the United States. Tall buildings with ledges resemble the cliffs on which peregrines naturally nest. And the large populations of starlings and pigeons offer a plentiful supply of food. Early in the morning, Baltimore residents can see Scarlet flying above their city, looking for prey. When she spots a pigeon, she dives at speeds of up to 150 miles per hour. She catches her victim in midair. Then, with the pigeon clasped tightly in her sharp talons, she turns and heads for her ledge, where she can enjoy a quiet breakfast.

The establishment of natural parks and nature reserves has also preserved species. Kirtland's warbler has been saved because government agencies set up special nesting areas for it in Michigan's Huron National Forest. This bird depends on fires to create the habitat it needs. After a fire destroys a forest, new vegetation soon begins to grow. One plant that develops on fire-blackened land is the jack pine. Kirtland's warbler will nest only in thickets of young jack pines. In addition, the ground must be covered with grasses that will conceal the bird's nest. After 10 to 15 years, the pines will have grown too tall to suit the warbler, and the bird will leave. Encroaching farms and other human developments have greatly decreased the number of jack-pine forests in Michigan. But in the national forest, controlled burning, the harvesting of trees, and other practices create exactly the right habitats for Kirtland's warbler.

Both **the ivory-billed woodpecker** (above) and **Kirtland's warbler** (right) are dependent upon forests for their food and shelter. When the forests are displaced by human settlements these birds lose their natural habitats and are threatened with extinction. The ivory-billed woodpecker may already be extinct.

Once a species is extinct, it is gone forever. It cannot be re-created. You will never see a live passenger pigeon or heath hen. Nor will you ever see a Tecopa pupfish again.

Will you—and your children, and your children's children—see tigers and pygmy hippopotamuses in the African wild? Will you be able to watch a whale swimming off the coast of California? Will you hear the booming sounds of courting prairie chickens or watch the antics of the ivory-billed woodpecker?

The time to answer these questions is now. All of us share the responsibility of seeing that the answer is yes. As members of the animal world ourselves, we have a stake in saving the other animals that share our planet.

The Florida manatee (or sea cow) is protected by law, but it still may be harmed as was this one that has scars on its side from a run-in with the propeller of a boat.

INDEX

This index includes some special features that make it an especially helpful tool in using this book. The plurals of words with unusual forms (usually Latin words) are indicated. Pronunciations are given here when the text includes them. The first entry tells you where a word or concept is defined in the book. References to photographs, art, diagrams, charts, or maps are indicated by *italic* type.